ADVANCED FRENCH
VOCABULARY

PHILIP HORSFALL

MARY GLASGOW PUBLICATIONS

First published in 1994 by:
Mary Glasgow Publications
An imprint of Stanley Thornes (Publishers) Ltd
Ellenborough House
Wellington Street
CHELTENHAM GL50 1YW
England

Reprinted 1995

A catalogue record for this book is available from the British Library.

ISBN 1 8523 4481 4

Typeset by Tech-Set, Gateshead, Tyne and Wear
Printed and bound in Great Britain at Redwood Books, Trowbridge, Wiltshire

TABLE DES MATIÈRES

AVANT-PROPOS

Ce livre a pour but:

- d'élargir votre vocabulaire en regroupant ensemble des mots sur des sujets d'intérêt général.
- de vous aider à écrire des dissertations en vous fournissant des phrases utiles.
- de vous préparer pour votre examen.
- de vous aider à apprendre tous ces mots en vous donnant des idées sur les meilleurs moyens de les assimiler.

Bien sûr, ce livre ne peut remplacer ni votre cahier de vocabulaire personnel où vous notez les mots que vous avez trouvés et dont vous avez besoin, ni un bon dictionnaire. Il peut, cependant, vous rendre la vie plus facile!
Je vous souhaite bonne chance!

Abbréviations:

adj	adjective	*mpl*	masculine plural
pl	plural	*fpl*	feminine plural
m	masculine	*m/f*	masculine and feminine
f	feminine	*m/fpl*	masculine and feminine plural

Les verbes irréguliers marqués # sont expliqués à la page 6.

Des adresses vous sont données pour vous aider à obtenir plus d'information si vous en avez besoin. Vous trouverez une lettre modèle pour demander plus de documentation à la page 58.

LA CULTURE

LA LITTÉRATURE

absorbant/e	*absorbing*
actuel/le	*topical*
ambigu/ë	*ambiguous*
auteur (*m*)	*author*
cadre (*m*)	*setting*
caractère (*m*)	*character, personality*
chapitre (*m*)	*chapter*
citer	*to quote*
clou (*m*)	*highlight*
conte (*m*)	*short story*
contrebalancer	*to offset*
convaincant/e	*convincing*
crise (*f*) de conscience	
	crisis of conscience
décrire#	*to describe*
déroulement (*m*)	*development*
dilemme (*m*) moral	*moral dilemma*
dominer	*to dominate*
éclairant/e	*enlightening*
écrivain (*m*)	*writer*
émouvant/e	*moving*
s'enchaîner	*to follow on, to be linked*
état (*m*) d'âme	*mood, frame of mind*
évoquer	*to call to mind*
s'exprimer	*to express oneself*
extrait (*m*)	*extract*
faire# allusion à	*to refer to*

faire# figure de	*to be regarded as*
fidèle	*accurate*
s'identifier avec	*to identify with*
intrigue (*f*)	*plot*
invraisemblable	*unbelievable*
milieu (*m*)	*environment, circle*
se montrer	*to show oneself as*
narrateur (*m*)	*narrator*
œuvre (*f*)	*work*
paradoxal/e	*paradoxical*
parallèle (*m*)	*parallel*
poète (*m*)	*poet*
point (*m*) culminant	*climax*
porter sur	*to focus on*
poussé/e par	*motivated by*
profondeur (*f*)	*depth*
psychologique	*psychological*
se rapporter à	*to tie in with*
réalisme (*m*)	*realism*
recréer	*to recreate*
résumé (*m*)	*summary*
révéler#	*to reveal*
roman (*m*)	*novel*
sentiment (*m*)	*feeling*
signification (*f*)	*meaning*
sort (*m*)	*fate*
souligner	*to stress*
stimulant/e	*thought-provoking*

sujet (*m*)	*subject matter*	trait (*m*)	*feature, trait*
susciter	*to arouse, give rise to*	traiter de	*to deal with*
symbolique	*symbolic*	se transformer	*to be a changed person*
tiraillé/e entre	*torn between*	vive	*vivid*

la peinture des caractères	*characterisation*
faire# progresser l'action	*to move the plot along*
il revient sur ce thème	*he comes back to this theme*
une étude des mœurs de	*a study of the manners/morals of*
éducation sentimentale	*romantic education*
faire# ressortir la morale	*to bring out the moral*
une composante essentielle de sa personnalité	*an essential side to his character*
notre intérêt se porte sur	*our interest focuses on*
à l'arrière-plan	*in the background*
la passion possède un pouvoir destructeur	*the power of passion is destructive*
écrit/e à la première personne	*written in the first person*
restituer l'époque de	*to reconstruct the period of*
les conséquences de ses actes	*the consequences of his actions*
soutenir# l'intérêt du lecteur par	*to hold the reader's interest by*

LE THÉÂTRE

acte (*m*)	*act*	incarner	*to embody*
comédien/ne (*m/f*)	*actor/actress*	interpréter#	*to perform*
dénouement (*m*)	*outcome, ending*	personnage (*m*)	*character, person*
dialogue (*m*)	*dialogue*	pièce (*f*)	*play*
dramaturge (*m*)	*playwright*	représenter	*to portray*
effet (*m*) scénique	*stage effect*	rôle (*m*)	*role, part*
entourage (*m*)	*circle, close group of people*	toile (*f*) de fond	*backcloth, backdrop*

3

se laisser entraîner par	*to let oneself be carried along by*
faire# progresser l'action	*to move the plot along*
l'action se déroule dans	*the action takes place in*
la scène se passe à	*the scene takes place at*
le sujet essentiel de la pièce	*the play's fundamental message*
les ressorts de l'action	*the forces behind the action*
mettre# en valeur ses idées sur	*to bring out clearly his ideas on*

LE CINÉMA

ambiance (*f*)	*atmosphere*
au ralenti	*in slow motion*
bande (*f*) sonore	*sound-track*
bruitage (*m*)	*sound effects*
censure (*f*)	*censorship*
cinéphile (*m/f*)	*film lover*
en gros plan	*in close-up*
figurant/e (*m/f*)	*extra*
film (*m*) à gros budget	*big budget film*
film (*m*) d'époque	*a period film*
film (*m*) noir	*social realism thriller*
générique (*m*)	*credits, cast-list*
s'inspirer de	*to be inspired by*
intimiste	*confiding*
long métrage (*m*)	*feature film*

metteur (*m*) en scène	*director*
nouvelle vague (*f*)	*French New Wave cinema*
panoramiquer	*to pan*
partenaires (*mpl*)	*supporting cast*
plateau (*m*) de tournage	*film set*
prise (*f*) de vue(s)	*filming, shooting*
réalisateur (*m*)	*producer*
rôle (*m*) principal	*leading role*
scénariste (*m/f*)	*script-writer*
scène (*f*)	*scene*
suite (*f*)	*sequel*
tournage (*m*)	*filming*
tourner	*to shoot*
truquage (*m*)	*special effects*
vedette (*f*)	*star*

retrouver ces thèmes dans d'autres films	*to come across these themes in other films*
enchaîner une série de films	*to link a series of films*
un film qui donne plus à penser qu'à voir	*a film that is more thought-provoking than visually interesting*
l'œuvre (*f*) filmique de	*the cinematic works of*
un film à succès	*a box-office success*
adapté/e pour le cinéma	*adapted for the cinema*
le film s'écarte du roman	*the film does not stick to the book*

LA MUSIQUE

air (*m*)	*melody*
batterie (*f*)	*percussion*
bois (*mpl*)	*woodwind*
chef (*m*) d'orchestre	*conductor*
compositeur (*m*)	*composer*
cuivres (*mpl*)	*brass instruments*
disque (*m*) compact	*CD*
folklorique	*folk*
instrument (*m*) à vent	*wind instrument*
instruments (*mpl*) à cordes	*strings*

interprétation (*f*)	*performance*
mélomane (*m/f*)	*music-lover*
musique (*f*) de fond	*background music*
opéra (*m*)	*opera*
orchestre (*m*)	*orchestra*
partition (*f*)	*score*
répéter#	*to rehearse*
tournée (*f*)	*tour*
tube (*m*)	*pop hit*
virtuose (*m/f*)	*virtuoso*

comporter quatre mouvements	*to be in four movements*
la musique adoucit les mœurs	*music has a civilising effect*
avoir# un énorme succès	*to be a big hit*
être# en tête du hit-parade	*to top the charts*

LES BEAUX-ARTS

abstrait/e	*abstract*
air (*m*)	*melody*
aquarelle (*f*)	*water-colour*
artisanat (*m*)	*arts and crafts*
assister à	*to attend*
choquant/e	*shocking*
curiosités (*fpl*)	*sights, features*
exposition (*f*)	*exhibition*
impressionnistes (*mpl*)	*the Impressionists*
laid/e	*ugly*
objet (*m*) d'art	*work of art*

patrimoine (*m*)	*cultural heritage*
peinture (*f*)	*painting*
peinture (*f*) à l'huile	*oil-painting*
philistin/e	*low-brow*
photographie (*f*)	*photography*
restaurer	*to restore*
sacré/e	*sacred*
sculpteur (*m*)	*sculptor*
sensibilité (*f*)	*sensitivity*
vitraux (*mpl*)	*stained glass windows*
vivant/e	*lifelike*
voûte (*f*)	*vault*

l'art pour l'art	*art for art's sake*
faire# des études d'art	*to study art*
l'art moderne semble dénué de sens	*modern art seems devoid of meaning*
c'est à déconseiller	*it's not to be recommended*

ADRESSES UTILES

Centre national de la cinématographie, 12 rue de Lubeck, 75116 Paris

Direction du livre et de la lecture, 27 avenue de l'Opéra, 75001 Paris

Fédération française des maisons de jeunes et de la culture, 15 rue la Condamine, 75017 Paris

Ministère de l'éducation et de la culture, 110 rue de Grenelles, 75357 Paris

Union des théâtres de l'Europe, Théâtre national de l'Odéon, 1 place Paul-Claudel, 75006 Paris

Union des jeunesses musicales d'Europe, rue royale 10, B-1000 Bruxelles

---

CONSEIL DE VOCABULAIRE

Rappel – Pour bien apprendre du vocabulaire, il faut faire quelque chose d'actif. C'est en forgeant qu'on devient forgeron!

Si le verbe est marqué #, cela vous signale qu'il est irrégulier et qu'il faut faire attention quand on l'utilise dans une phrase. Il vaut mieux vérifier dans votre dictionnaire pour trouver la forme nécessaire. Par exemple:

	Present	*Imperfect*	*Perfect*	*Future*	
venir	**je viens**	**je venais**	**je suis venu**	**je viendrai**	etc.

(voir la page 12 des appendices du *Dictionnaire Français-Anglais Collins Robert 3ème édition*)

L'ÉCONOMIE

LE COMMERCE

achat (*m*)	purchase
association (*f*)	partnership
avoir (*m*)	credit note
biens (*mpl*)	goods
braderie (*f*)	cut-price goods
commerçant (*m*)	shopkeeper
chaîne (*f*) de montage	assembly line
clientèle (*f*)	customers
commander	to order
consommateur (*m*)	consumer
détaillant (*m*)	retailer
emballage (*m*)	wrapping
entreprise (*f*)	firm
exportation (*f*)	export
fabrication (*f*)	manufacture
fabriquer	to manufacture
facture (*f*)	bill, invoice
faire# faillite	to go bankrupt
filiale (*f*)	subsidiary office
foire (*f*)	trade fair
gamme (*f*) de produits	product range

grande surface (*f*)	hypermarket
guerre (*f*) des prix	price war
heures (*fpl*) ouvrables	business hours
hiérarchie (*f*)	company structure
importation (*f*)	import
lettre (*f*) commerciale	business letter
livrer	to deliver
marchandises (*fpl*)	goods
petit commerçant (*m*)	small shopkeeper
point (*m*) de vente	sales outlet
produit (*m*)	product
promotion (*f*)	special offer
rabais (*m*)	reduction
réclamation (*f*)	complaint
relations (*fpl*) du travail	industrial relations
rembourser	to refund
service (*m*) après-vente	after-sales service
siège (*m*)	headquarters
succursale (*f*)	branch
vente (*f*) en gros	wholesale trade

délaisser les commerces de quartier	to abandon local shops
augmenter/baisser les prix	to increase/reduce prices
un centre commercial représente un apport d'emplois	a shopping centre brings with it jobs
se situer dans les zones périurbaines	to be located on the outskirts of towns

vérifier la date limite de vente	*to check the sell-by date*
effectuer un achat	*to make a purchase*
dans un rayon de 20 kilomètres	*within a 20 kilometre radius*
il y a un manque d'accueil	*the personal touch is missing*
faire# des affaires sur une grande échelle	*to do business on a large scale*
la livraison à domicile	*home delivery*
faire# face à la concurrence	*to stand up to the competition*
répondre# aux besoins des clients	*to meet the customers' needs*
une société anonyme	*public limited company*
les affaires reprennent	*business is looking up*

LA BANQUE

agence (*f*)	*branch*
argent (*m*) liquide	*cash*
billetterie (*f*)	*cash dispenser*
brut	*gross*
Carte (*f*) Bleue	*Visa card*
carte (*f*) de crédit	*credit card*
carte (*f*) de retrait	*cashcard*
compte (*m*) courant	*current account*
compte (*m*) d'épargne	*savings account*
découvert (*m*)	*overdraft*
devises (*fpl*)	*foreign currency*
directeur (*m*) d'agence	*bank manager*

distributeur (*m*) de billets	*cash dispenser*
épargnant/e (*m/f*)	*saver*
espèces (*fpl*)	*cash*
frais (*mpl*) de banque	*banking charges*
hypothèque (*f*)	*mortgage*
intérêts (*mpl*)	*interest*
net	*net*
point (*m*) argent	*cash point*
relevé (*m*) de compte	*statement*
retirer	*to withdraw*
secteur (*m*) bancaire	*banking industry*
société (*f*) sans argent	*cashless society*
virer	*to transfer*

toucher un chèque	*to cash a cheque*
verser de l'argent sur un compte	*to pay money into an account*
le taux de change	*exchange rate*
le taux d'intérêt	*the interest rate*
atteindre# son niveau le plus bas	*to reach an all-time low*
en francs constants	*in real terms*

LES FINANCES

bénéfice (*m*)	*profit*
budget (*m*)	*budget*
charge (*f*) fiscale	*tax burden*
chiffre (*m*) d'affaires	*turnover*
contribuable *(m/f)*	*taxpayer*
dette (*f*) (publique)	*(national) debt*
dépense (*f*)	*expenditure*
économie (*f*) parallèle	
	black economy
endetté/e	*in debt*
financement (*m*)	*finance*
fiscalité (*f*)	*taxation*
fraude (*f*) fiscale	*tax evasion*

hausse (*f*) des prix	*price rise*
impôt (*m*) sur le revenu	*income tax*
inflationniste	*inflationary*
milliard (*m*)	*billion*
perception (*f*)	*tax office*
placement (*m*)	*investment*
pourcentage (*m*)	*percentage*
prix (*m*) de revient	*cost price*
recettes (fpl) fiscales	*tax revenue*
reçu (*m*)	*receipt*
rentabilité (*f*)	*profitability*
taux (*m*) d'inflation	*rate of inflation*
TVA (*f*)	*VAT*
valeur (*f*) marchande	*market value*

donner du tonus à l'économie	*to boost the economy*
le mécanisme de change	*the exchange rate mechanism*
réduire# le déficit budgétaire	*to reduce the budget deficit*
la relance économique	*the economic revival*
favoriser la croissance	*to encourage growth*

DIVERS

action (*f*)	*share*
actionnaire *(m/f)*	*shareholder*
boom (*m*)	*boom*
bourse (*f*)	*stock exchange*
conjoncture (*f*)	*state of the economy*
crise (*f*)	*crisis*
effondrement (*m*)	*slump*
forces (*fpl*) du marché	*market forces*

krach (*m*)	*stock-market crash*
libre-échange (*m*)	*free-trade*
passage (*m*) à la baisse	
	downward trend
perspectives (*fpl*)	*prospects*
placer	*to invest*
privatiser	*to privatise*
récession (*f*)	*recession*
spéculer	*to speculate*
surchauffe (*f*)	*overheating*

9

le cours des actions est monté	*the share price has risen*
les exportations invisibles	*invisible exports*
les marchés financiers	*financial markets*
le déficit commercial	*the trade gap*
la balance des paiements	*the balance of payments*
la balance commerciale	*the balance of trade*
les résultats financiers	*trade figures*
l'indice du coût de la vie	*the cost of living index*
un délit d'initié	*insider dealing*

ADRESSES UTILES

Chambre de commerce de Paris, 27 avenue de Friedland, Paris

Banque Nationale de Paris, 16 boulevard des Italiens, 75009 Paris

Ministère de l'économie, 13 rue Saint-Georges, 75436 Paris

Institut national de la consommation, 80 rue Lecourbe, 75015 Paris

Association française des banques, 18 rue Lafayette, 75009 Paris

Société des bourses françaises, 4 place de la Bourse, 75080 Paris

Les chambres françaises de commerce et d'industrie, 45 avenue d'Iéna, 75116 Paris

CONSEIL DE VOCABULAIRE

Rappel – Pour bien apprendre du vocabulaire, il faut faire quelque chose d'actif. C'est en forgeant qu'on devient forgeron!

Comment peut-on deviner si un mot est masculin ou féminin? Il y a quelques règles en ce qui concerne les terminaisons (mais vous trouverez toujours quelques rares exceptions!).

Masculin:

-ment   e.g établissement, effondrement, placement

-a   e.g. opéra, brouhaha, panorama

-é   e.g. marché, péché, sinistré

-i   e.g. cri, abri, ennui

-age   e.g. emballage, orage, reportage

-ier   e.g. boutiquier, chantier, immobilier

-acle   e.g. miracle, obstacle, spectacle

-ège   e.g. collège, privilège, cortège

-ème   e.g. problème, thème, système

-isme   e.g. snobisme, communisme, mécanisme

Féminin:

-ion   e.g. promotion, réclamation, action

-oire   e.g. gloire, victoire, baignoire

-té   e.g. bonté, félicité, inégalité

-tié   e.g. amitié, pitié, moitié

-ison   e.g. guérison, raison, pendaison

-ique   e.g. statistique, critique, politique

-ière   e.g. croisière, lisière, portière

L'ENSEIGNEMENT

AU COLLÈGE

absentéisme (*m*)	*truancy*
ardu/e	*very difficult*
assidu/e	*hard-working*
bonne conduite (*f*)	*good behaviour*
bulletin (*m*) scolaire	*report*
chahuter	*to run riot*
classe-poubelle (*f*)	*sink group*
collégien/ne (*m/f*)	*pupil*
connaissance (*f*)	*knowledge*
cours (*m*) particulier	*private lesson*
directeur/trice (*m/f*)	*headteacher*
discipline (*f*)	*discipline*
en première	*in Year 12*
en terminale	*in Year 13*
école (*f*) libre	*private school*
école (*f*) publique	*state school*
élitisme (*m*)	*elitism*

illettré/e	*illiterate*
internat (*m*)	*boarding school*
mixte	*mixed*
obligatoire	*compulsory*
orientation (*f*)	*guidance*
pédagogique	*educational*
pluridisciplinaire	*cross-curricular*
programme (*m*) scolaire	*curriculum*
rattraper	*to catch up*
redoubler	*to repeat a year*
renvoyé/e	*suspended, expelled*
réunion (*f*) de profs	*staff meeting*
sagesse (*f*)	*good behaviour*
scolarité (*f*)	*schooling*
sortie (*f*) scolaire	*school trip*
surchargé/e	*overloaded*
surveillant/e (*m/f*)	*supervisor*

l'enseignement laïque	*state education*
la formation est la clé de l'avenir	*education is the key to the future*
le système éducatif	*the educational system*
une dégradation des niveaux	*a drop in standards*
prolonger# la scolarité	*to raise the school-leaving age*
le taux d'encadrement	*the staff-pupil ratio*
un dossier scolaire	*school record*
la pesanteur administrative	*the administrative burden*

le programme d'enseignement obligatoire	*the national curriculum*
l'âge de la fin de la scolarité	*school-leaving age*
le premier cycle	*education from 11–13*
le second cycle court	*education from 14–16*
les activités extra-scolaires	*out of school activities*
l'état des locaux	*the state of the buildings*
les voyages forment la jeunesse	*travel broadens young people's minds*

LES EXAMENS

appréciation (*f*)	*assessment*
baccalauréat (*m*)	*A-level equivalent*
bachelier/ière (*m/f*)	
	someone who has the 'bac'
bachoter	*to swot, cram*
concours (*m*)	*competition*
contrôle (*m*) continu	
	continuous assessment
échec (*m*)	*failure*
échouer à	*to fail*
écrit/e	*written*
épreuve (*f*)	*test*

équitable	*fair*
interrogation (*f*)	*test*
oral/e	*oral, verbal*
passer un examen	*to take an exam*
pratique	*practical*
résultat (*m*)	*result*
réussir à	*to pass*
réviser	*to revise*
sélectionner	*to select*
sésame (*m*)	*key to*
succès (*m*)	*success*
théorique	*theoretical*
tricher	*to cheat*

le bac est le sésame à la faculté	*the 'bac' is the key to a university place*
avoir# un trou de mémoire	*to have your mind go blank*
la sélection par l'échec	*to weed out by examination*
la valeur intrinsèque de	*the intrinsic merit of*
se sentir# bloqué/e	*to have a mental block*
décrocher le bac	*to gain the 'bac'*
les diplômes scolaires	*educational qualifications*

13

APRÈS LE COLLÈGE

amphithéâtre (*m*)	*lecture hall*
approfondir	*to deepen*
bourse (*f*)	*grant*
CAPES (*m*)	*teaching diploma*
club (*m*) des étudiants	*students' union*
cours (*m*)	*lecture*
cours (*m*) du soir	*evening class*
se cultiver	*to improve one's mind*
cursus (*m*)	*degree course*
diplôme (*m*)	*qualification*
diplômé/e	*qualified*
directeur/trice (*m/f*) d'études	*tutor*
doctorat (*m*)	*Ph.D.*
École polytechnique (*f*)	*specialist college*

faculté (*f*)	*university*
formation (*f*)	*training*
Grandes Écoles (*fpl*)	*prestigious, specialist universities*
s'instruire#	*to educate oneself*
licence (*f*)	*degree*
licencié/e (*m/f*)	*graduate*
maîtrise (*f*)	*MA*
recherche (*f*)	*research*
recteur (*m*)	*vice-chancellor*
semestre (*m*)	*semester*
stagiaire (*m/f*)	*trainee*
thèse (*f*)	*thesis*
travaux (*mpl*) dirigés	*tutorial*
trimestre (*m*)	*term*
universitaire	*university (adj)*

la vie estudiantine	*student life*
la cité universitaire	*hall of residence*
poursuivre# ses études	*to continue with one's studies*
faire# cours sur	*to lecture on*
la formation pédagogique	*teacher training*
la formation en alternance	*sandwich course*
s'inscrire# à un cours	*to register for a course*
le concours d'entrée à	*competitive entrance examination for*
une classe préparatoire	*group preparing for entrance exams*
l'école normale supérieure	*specialist teacher training college*

ADRESSES UTILES

Ministère de l'éducation nationale, 110 rue de Grenelle, 75357 Paris

Centre national de documentation pédagogique, 29 rue d'Ulm, 75230 Paris

Centre national d'enseignement à distance, Tour Paris-Lyon, 209-211 rue de Bercy, 75585 Paris

Documentation statistique, Sprese 7, 58 boulevard du Lycée, 92170 Vanves

Librairie d'information sur les enseignements et les professions, 168 boulevard du Montparnasse, 75014, Paris

Librairie du centre national de documentation pédagogique, 13 rue du Four, 75006 Paris

CONSEIL DE VOCABULAIRE

Rappel – Pour bien apprendre du vocabulaire, il faut faire quelque chose d'actif. C'est en forgeant qu'on devient forgeron!

Jouez au loto! Pas avec les numéros mais avec les mots! Quand vous avez appris une vingtaine de mots de cette section du livre, vous en écrivez huit au hasard en français sur un bout de papier. Puis vous demandez à un(e) partenaire de lire à haute voix quatorze mots au hasard en anglais de votre liste de vingt mots. Cochez les mots que vous entendez – avez-vous bien choisi? Si oui, vous dites «loto!».

L'ENVIRONNEMENT

LE TRANSPORT

aérien/ne	air (adj)
Alcootest (m)	Breathalyser
annulation (f)	cancellation
atterrir	to land
automobiliste (m/f)	motorist
avion (m) à réaction	jet aircraft
blocus (m)	blockade
bouchon (m)	traffic jam
boutique (f) hors taxe	duty-free shop
bruyant/e	noisy
capacité (f)	capacity
carambolage (m)	pile up
carlingue (f)	aircraft cabin
ceinture (f) de sécurité	seatbelt
charter (m)	charter flight
chauffard (m)	roadhog
chemin (m) de fer	railway
circulation (f)	traffic
circuler	to run
code (m) de la route	highway code
compagnie (f) aérienne	airline
contraignant/e	restricting
contravention (f)	fine
couloir (m) de bus	bus lane
décoller	to take off
décongestionner	to relieve congestion
délai (m)	delay

efficace	efficient
embouteillage (m)	traffic jam
excès (m) de vitesse	speeding
faire# de l'autostop	to hitch-hike
ferroviaire	railway (adj)
garer	to park
grands axes (mpl)	main roads
heures (fpl) de pointe	rush hours
horaire (m)	timetable
incommode	inconvenient
long-courrier	long-haul (aircraft)
mal (m) de l'air	airsickness
navette (f)	shuttle
péage (m)	toll
périphérique (m)	ring road
permis (m) de conduire	driving licence
piste (f) cyclable	cycle lane
poids (m) lourd	heavy goods vehicle
rame (f)	underground train
rapidité (f)	speed
relier	to link
retardé/e	delayed
réseau (m) autoroutier	motorway network
rouler	to drive along
routier (m)	lorry driver
rues (fpl) piétonnes	pedestrianised streets

sécurité (f) routière	road safety
subvention (f)	subsidy
trajet (m)	journey

se véhiculer	to get around
voiture (f) particulière	private car
zone (f) piétonne	pedestrian precinct

emprunter les transports en commun	to use public transport
une ville bien desservie	a town with a good transport system
le parc (m) automobile	the number of vehicles on the road
rétrécir les distances	to shrink distances
un investissement dans l'infrastructure	an investment in the infrastructure
l'hécatombe sur les routes	the carnage on the roads

LE TEMPS

s'améliorer	to improve
brouillard (m) givrant	freezing fog
brume (f)	mist
canicule (f)	heatwave
chute (f) de neige	snowfall
couvert	cloudy, overcast
se dégager	to clear
éclaircie (f)	sunny spell

s'éclaircir	to clear up
ensoleillé/e	sunny
flocon (m) de neige	snowflake
intempéries (fpl)	bad weather
maussade	gloomy
mistral (m)	mistral wind
venteux/euse	windy
verglas (m)	black ice

des températures douces pour la saison	mild temperatures for the time of year
des risques d'averses	chance of showers
le climat est soumis à	the climate is subject to
des fronts chauds	warm fronts

LES DÉCHETS

| broyeur (m) d'ordures | waste disposal unit |
| consigne (f) | deposit |

conteneur (m) vert	bottle bank
décharge (f)	dump
dépotoire (m)	rubbish tip
éboueur (m)	refuse collector

élimination (*f*) des déchets
waste disposal

gestion (*f*) des déchets
waste management

nettoyage (*m*) *clean-up*

ordures (*f*) *household waste*

ramassage (*m*) d'ordures
rubbish collection

récupérable *reclaimable*

récupération (*f*)
salvaging, reprocessing

réutilisable *reusable*

site (*m*) vierge *green-field site*

tas (*m*) de compost *compost heap*

trier *to separate out*

usine (*f*) de traitement
recycling plant

le papier recyclé — *recycled paper*

une bouteille consignée — *a bottle with a deposit*

avoir# des conséquences redoutables — *to have dreadful consequences*

la dépollution des plages — *cleaning up the beaches*

L'ÉNERGIE

carburant (*m*) *fuel*

centrale (*f*) nucléaire
nuclear power station

charbon (*m*) *coal*

combustible (*m*) organique *biofuel*

combustibles (*mpl*) fossiles *fossil fuels*

déchets (*m*) nucléaires *nuclear waste*

désactiver *to deactivate*

diversifier *to diversify*

économies (*f*) d'énergie
energy savings

énergie (*f*) éolienne *wind power*

énergie (*f*) solaire *solar power*

houille (*f*) blanche
hydro-electric power

inépuisable *inexhaustible*

politique (*f*) énergétique
energy policy

problème (*m*) énergétique
the energy problem

remplacer *to replace*

ressources (*f*) naturelles
natural resources

risque (*m*) nucléaire *nuclear risk*

usine (*f*) marémotrice
tidal power station

trouver des énergies douces	*to find safe energy sources*
des énergies (*f*) renouvelables	*renewable energy sources*
enrayer# la menace nucléaire	*to stop the nuclear threat*
répondre# aux besoins énergétiques	*to meet the energy requirements*
provenir# du nucléaire	*to come from nuclear energy*
utilisé/e à des fins pacifiques	*used for peaceful purposes*

LES DROITS DES ANIMAUX

abattoir (*m*)	*slaughterhouse*
agoniser	*to be dying*
anesthésier	*to anaesthetise*
animalerie (*f*)	*animal house*
animaux (*mpl*) de boucherie	*fatstock, animals killed for meat*
s'apitoyer sur	*to feel pity for*
atroce	*atrocious*
baleine (*f*)	*whale*
bébé-phoque (*m*)	*baby seal*
bête (*f*) de boucherie	*animal for slaughter*
bien-fondé (*m*)	*validity*
braconnage (*m*)	*poaching*
chasse (*f*)	*hunting*

cible (*f*)	*target*
cobaye (*m*)	*guinea pig (in experiment)*
dompter	*to tame*
dresser	*to train*
élevage (*m*)	*rearing, breeding*
extinction (*f*)	*extinction*
faune (*f*)	*wildlife*
gibier (*m*)	*game*
guetter	*to lie in wait for*
humain/e	*humane*
mammifère (*m*)	*mammal*
menacer#	*to threaten*
piéger#	*to trap*
rage (*f*)	*rabies*
sport (*m*) sanguinaire	*blood-sport*
vivisection (*f*)	*vivisection*

la cruauté envers les animaux	*cruelty to animals*
le commerce illégal de l'ivoire	*the illegal trade in ivory*
l'expérimentation animale	*experiments on animals*
la chasse baleinière commerciale	*commercial whaling*
le défenseur des droits des animaux	*animal rights activist*
la préservation de la baleine	*saving the whale*

les espèces menacées — *threatened species*

infliger# des souffrances à — *to inflict suffering on*

préconiser l'arrêt total de — *to be in favour of a total ban on*

l'expérience médicale — *medical experiment*

DIVERS

azote (*m*) — *nitrogen*

biodégradable — *biodegradable*

bombe (*f*) aérosol — *aerosol spray*

CFC (*mpl*) — *CFCs*

contaminé/e — *contaminated*

couche (*f*) d'ozone — *ozone layer*

déboiser — *to deforest*

désertification (*f*) — *turning into a desert*

écolo — *green*

écologique — *ecological*

effet (*m*) de serre — *greenhouse effect*

emballage (*m*) — *packaging*

engrais (*m*) chimique — *artificial fertiliser*

essence (*f*) sans plomb — *lead-free petrol*

gaspillage (*m*) — *wastage*

gaz (*m*) carbonique — *carbon dioxide*

logo (*m*) vert — *green label*

marée (*f*) noire — *large oil slick*

nappe (*f*) de pétrole — *small oil slick*

oxyde (*m*) de carbone — *carbon monoxide*

pluie (*f*) acide — *acid rain*

polluer — *to pollute*

pollution (*f*) des eaux — *water pollution*

pot (*m*) catalytique — *catalytic converter*

produit (*m*) bio — *organically grown product*

rayons (*mpl*) ultraviolets — *ultra-violet rays*

recyclage (*m*) — *recycling*

se réchauffer — *to heat up*

sauvegarde (*f*) — *safeguard*

toxique — *poisonous*

le réchauffement de la planète — *global warming*

une lessive aux enzymes — *a biological washing powder*

les glaces polaires se fondent — *the polar ice-caps are melting*

le niveau des océans remonte — *the sea-level is rising*

qui ne nuit pas à l'environnement — *environmentally friendly*

défricher les forêts tropicales — *to cut down rainforests*

dégrader l'environnement	*to damage the environment*
les questions écologiques	*green issues*
faire# prendre conscience aux gens	*to raise people's consciousness*
un groupe de pression écologiste	*environmental pressure group*
le risque pour la santé	*health hazard*
les Amis de la Terre	*Friends of the Earth*
le phosphate asphyxie les rivières	*phosphates are choking the rivers*
les nappes d'eaux souterraines	*underground water tables*
faire# rimer l'écologie et l'économie	*to mix the environment and the economy sensibly*
les matières premières	*raw materials*
un défenseur de l'environnement	*a conservationist*

ADRESSES UTILES

Agence française pour la maîtrise de l'énergie, 27 rue Louis Vicat, 75737 Paris

Fédération française des sociétés de la protection de la nature, 57 rue Cuvier, 75005 Paris

Centre d'information sur le bruit, 4 rue Beffroy, 92200 Neuilly-sur-Seine

Ligue contre la violence routière, 5 Impasse Bon-Secours, 75011 Paris

Rue de l'avenir, 18 rue de Varenne, 75007 Paris

Ministère de l'environnement, 14 boulevard du Général Leclerc, 92524 Neuilly-sur-Seine

Maison de l'énergie et de l'environnement, 15 rue du Louvre, 75001 Paris

Ligue française des droits de l'animal, 61 rue du Cherche Midi, 75006 Paris

Ligue française contre la vivisection, 84 rue Blanche, 75009 Paris

Société protectrice des animaux, 39 boulevard Berthier, 75017 Paris

Groupement des autorités responsables de transport, 77 boulevard du Montparnasse, 75006 Paris

CONSEIL DE VOCABULAIRE

Rappel – Pour bien apprendre du vocabulaire, il faut faire quelque chose d'actif. C'est en forgeant qu'on devient forgeron!

Employez la technologie pour vous aider! Par exemple, enregistrez sur une cassette les mots et les phrases que vous trouvez utiles dans cette section du livre.

Par exemple: le trou dans la couche d'ozone (pause)   hole in the ozone layer.

l'effet de serre (pause)   greenhouse effect , etc.

Vous l'écoutez plusieurs fois, puis vous enclenchez la touche pause et vous essayez de dire l'anglais avant la bande. Vous pouvez même essayer de répondre sans arrêter la bande! Puis vous faites l'inverse – vous enregistrez l'anglais d'abord, puis le français . Si vous n'aimez pas votre propre voix, échangez de cassette avec un partenaire!

N'oubliez pas non plus les ordinateurs. Inventez un jeu sur votre ordinateur pour réviser les mots. Beaucoup des conseils de vocabulaire dans ce livre pourraient être transférés sur un ordinateur.

LES ÉTRANGERS

LES GENS

allogène	*non-native*
autochtone	*native*
Beur (*m*)	*second generation North African immigrant*
cohabitation (*f*)	*living together*
concitoyen/ne (*m/f*)	*fellow citizen*
étranger/ère (*m/f*)	*foreigner*
habitants (*mpl*) du pays	*resident population*
immigrant/e (*m/f*)	*immigrant*
immigré/e (*m/f*)	*immigrant*

indigène	*local, indigenous*
Maghrébin/e (*m/f*)	*North African*
personnes (*fpl*) de couleur	*black and Asian people*
population (*f*) de couleur	*black and Asian population*
réfugié/e (*m/f*)	*refugee*
ressortissant/e (*m/f*)	*national*
sans-papiers (*m*)	*illegal immigrant*
société (*f*) pluriculturelle	*multicultural society*
visiteur/euse (*m/f*)	*visitor*

le brassage de races	*the intermixing of races*
un groupe ethnique minoritaire	*an ethnic minority*
les immigrés clandestins	*illegal immigrants*
vivre# en bonne harmonie	*to live together harmoniously*
un Français à part entière	*a fully-fledged French citizen*
les immigrés de la deuxième génération	*second-generation immigrants*
se sentir# mal à l'aise	*to feel ill at ease*

L'IMMIGRATION

ascension (*f*) sociale	*social advancement*
asile (*m*) politique	*political asylum*
assimilation (*f*)	*absorption*
camp (*m*) de réfugiés	*refugee camp*
carte (*f*) de séjour	*residence permit*

carte (*f*) de travail	*work permit*
chercher asile	*to seek asylum*
choc (*m*) culturel	*culture shock*
cité (*f*) de transit	*temporary hostel*
citoyenneté (*f*)	*citizenship*
désorienté/e	*bewildered*
s'entr'aider	*to help each other*

ethnique	*ethnic*
s'expatrier	*to leave one's country*
fixation (*f*)	*settling*
flux (*m*) migratoire	
	flood of immigrants
foyer (*m*)	*hostel*
ghetto (*m*)	*ghetto*
Hexagone (*m*)	*France*
inadapté/e	*not fitting in*
insertion (*f*)	*integration*
s'intégrer	*to fit in*

Maghreb (*m*)	*North Africa*
mode (*m*) de vie	*way of life*
naturalisation (*f*)	*naturalisation*
pays (*m*) d'adoption	*adopted country*
pays (*m*) d'origine	*country of origin*
pays (*m*) natal	*country of birth*
pièce (*f*) d'identité	*identity card*
refouler	*to turn back, refuse entry*
résider	*to be resident*
terre (*f*) d'accueil	*host country*
visa (*m*)	*visa*

renier leurs coutumes	*to give up their customs*
abuser de l'hospitalité	*to take unfair advantage of hospitality*
demander le droit d'asile	*to ask for political asylum*
bénéficier des droits sociaux	*to get social security*
être# en situation irrégulière	*to be breaking the law*
réglementer l'immigration	*to control immigration*
renier leurs racines	*to deny their roots*
le regroupement familial	*reuniting a family*
entrer en fraude	*to enter illegally*

LE RACISME

brute (*m*)	*bully*
comportement (*m*)	*race riot*
extrême droite (*f*)	*far right*
Front (*m*) national	*National Front*
gêner quelqu'un	*to bother someone*
grief (*m*)	*grievance*
harcèlement (*m*) policier	
	police harassment

intensification (*f*)	*escalation*
intolérance (*f*)	*intolerance*
matamore (*m*)	*bully*
méfiance (*f*)	*distrust*
mobile (*m*)	*motive*
opprimer	*to oppress*
pagaille (*f*)	*chaos*
parti (*m*) fasciste	*Fascist party*
racisme (*m*)	*racism*

se radicaliser	*to intensify*
railler	*to taunt*
rancœur (*f*)	*resentment*
ratonnade (*f*)	*attack on immigrants*
rejeter#	*to reject*

relations (*fpl*) inter-raciales	*race relations*
violence (*f*) raciste	*racial violence*
voyou (*m*)	*hooligan*
xénophobie (*f*)	*hatred of foreigners*

avoir# des préjugés racistes	*to be racially prejudiced*
le seuil de tolérance	*the threshold of tolerance*
la commission chargée de supprimer la discrimination raciale	*race relations board*
attiser les passions	*to stir up feelings*
l'escalade du racisme	*the escalation in racism*
une attaque raciste	*racially-motivated attack*
le traitement préférentiel	*preferential treatment*
sa couleur joue contre lui	*his colour counts against him*
le racisme n'est pas une opinion, c'est un délit	*racism isn't an opinion, it's a crime*
la recrudescence du racisme	*the upsurge in racism*
la montée de l'extrême droite	*the rise of the far right*
renvoyer# les immigrés chez eux	*to send immigrants back home*
la banalisation des idées racistes	*the commonplace acceptance of racist ideas*
désamorcer# la montée du racisme	*to counteract the increase in racism*
les idées lepénistes	*Le Pen's extreme right-wing ideas*

DIVERS

binational/e	*holding dual nationality*
collectivité (*f*)	*the community*
diversité (*f*) culturelle	*cultural diversity*
droits (*mpl*) de l'homme	*human rights*

édifice (*m*) social	*social fabric*
expulser	*to expel*
idée (*f*) erronée	*false idea*
inassimilable	*unable to be assimilated*
laxisme (*m*)	*being too soft*
marginalisé/e	*edged out, ignored*

mariage (*m*) de convenance		pluriracial/e	*multiracial*
marriage of convenience		repatriement (*m*)	*repatriation*
mœurs (*fpl*) locales	*local customs*	réprimer	*to crack down on*
ouvertement	*openly*		

améliorer les relations entre	*to improve relationships between*
à cheval entre deux sociétés	*to be split between two societies*
faire# un effort d'adaptation	*to try to adapt*
la patrie d'élection	*the country of one's own choosing*
rechercher la concertation avec	*to seek a dialogue with*
de souche française	*of old French stock*
une famille étendue	*extended family*
d'après la rumeur publique	*according to popular belief*

ADRESSES UTILES

Office national d'immigration, 44 rue Bargue, 75015 Paris

SOS Racisme, 19 rue Martel, 75010 Paris

Ministère de l'intérieur et de la sécurité publique, Place Beauvau, 75008 Paris

France Terre d'Asile, 4 passage Louis Philippe, 75011 Paris

UNHCR, Palais des Nations, Geneva, Switzerland

CONSEIL DE VOCABULAIRE

Rappel – Pour bien apprendre du vocabulaire, il faut faire quelque chose d'actif. C'est en forgeant qu'on devient forgeron!

Essayez d'apprendre les mots en faisant des phrases en français, mais en remplaçant quelques mots en anglais. Par exemple:

On ne peut pas (reject) sa patrie, mais également il faut faire un effort d' (adapting) à la nouvelle patrie d' (choosing).

Relisez vos phrases quelques jours plus tard. Pouvez-vous recopier la phrase avec les bons mots français? Par exemple:

On ne peut pas renier sa patrie, mais également il faut faire un effort d'adaptation à la nouvelle patrie d'élection.

LA FRANCE

UNE RÉGION DE LA FRANCE

accidenté/e	hilly
accueil (m)	welcome
arriéré/e	backward
arrière-pays (m)	hinterland
aspect (m) touristique	touristy side
atmosphère (f)	atmosphere
bassin (m)	basin
cadre (m) de vie	living environment
caractéristique (f)	characteristic
carnaval (m)	carnival
commémorer	to commemorate
se concentrer	to be concentrated
connu/e	well-known
contraste (m)	contrast
cultivable	suitable for growing
démuni/e	deprived
dépendant/e de	dependent on
développement (m)	development
doté/e de	endowed with
dynamisme (m)	dynamism
économie (f) diversifiée	varied economy
économie (f) régionale	regional economy
s'enorgueillir de	to pride itself on

ensoleillement (m)	hours of sunshine
essor (m)	expansion
facteur (m)	factor
faiblesse (f)	weakness
fier/ière de	proud of
florissant/e	flourishing
forestier/ière	forest (adj)
habitat (m)	habitat
haut lieu (m) de	Mecca for
image (f) de marque	public image
industrie (f) de pointe	high-tech industry
kermesse (f)	fair
littoral (m)	shore, coast
médiéval/e	medieval
mélange (m)	mixture
méridional/e	southern
Midi (m)	South of France
patrimoine (m)	heritage
paysage (m)	countryside
peuplé/e	populated
pluviosité (f)	average rainfall
se promotionner	to promote itself
prospérité (f)	wealth
région (f) à problème	problem area
relief (m)	contours, relief
renommé/e pour	famous for
reprise (f)	recovery, revival

richesses (*fpl*)	*riches, wealth*
secteur (*m*) tertiaire	*service industries*
sophistiqué/e	*sophisticated*
spécificité (*f*)	*distinctive feature*
témoigner de	*to indicate, bear witness to*
traditionnel/le	*traditional*

typique	*typical*
se vanter de	*to boast, be proud of*
vestiges (*mpl*) historiques	*historical remains*
ville (*f*) universitaire	*university town*
vitalité (*f*)	*vitality*
viticole	*wine-growing*

garder son identité unique	*to keep its unique identity*
sa situation géographique privilégiée	*its favoured geographical position*
la flore et la faune	*the plant and animal life*
une province à vocation agricole	*an agricultural province*
les particularismes régionaux	*regional idiosyncracies*
la douceur de son climat	*the mildness of its climate*
la disparition des industries traditionnelles	*the disappearance of traditional industries*
dépasser la moyenne nationale	*to be above the national average*
refléter# la puissance passée de	*to mirror the former power of*
disposer d'atouts considérables	*to have some considerable advantages*
attirer des entreprises	*to attract businesses*
ce qui caractérise ce paysage	*the main features of this landscape*
c'est une région durement touchée par	*it's an area badly affected by*
vivre# une profonde mutation	*to undergo profound changes*
un site naturel	*an area of outstanding natural beauty*
la région bénéficie de	*the area benefits from*

LA RÉSISTANCE

acte (*m*) fondateur	*founding action*
Allemagne (*f*) nazie	*Nazi Germany*
alliés (*mpl*)	*the Allies*

appareil (*m*) policier	*police machinery*
apport (*m*)	*contribution*
armée (*f*) des ombres	*secret army*
armée (*f*) occupante	*army of occupation*

armée (*f*) souterraine
underground army

armistice (*m*) — *armistice*

arrestation (*f*) — *arrest*

attentat (*m*) — *attack*

attentisme (*m*) — *wait and see policy*

balisage (*m*) — *marking out*

belligérant (*m*) — *nation at war*

camp (*m*) de concentration
concentration camp

capitulation (*f*) — *surrender*

cesser le combat — *to stop fighting*

clandestin/e — *secret*

clandestinité (*f*) — *resistance*

collaborateur/trice (*m/f*) — *collaborator*

collaboration (*f*) — *collaboration*

combattant/e (*m/f*) — *combatant*

coordonner — *to co-ordinate*

couvre-feu (*m*) — *curfew*

croix (*f*) gammée — *swastika*

défaite (*f*) — *defeat*

délivrer la France — *to set France free*

démoralisation (*f*) — *demoralisation*

dénonciation (*f*) — *exposure, betrayal*

déportation (*f*) — *internment, imprisonment in a concentration camp*

déporté/e (*m/f*) — *internee, person sent to a concentration camp*

détachement (*m*) — *detachment*

diffuser — *to spread, distribute*

dirigeant /e (*m/f*) — *leader*

drôle (*m*) de guerre — *phoney war*

en exil (*m*) — *in exile*

encercler — *to surround*

envahisseur (*m*) — *invader*

s'évader — *to escape*

faux papiers (*mpl*) — *forged papers*

forces (*fpl*) allemandes — *German forces*

franc-tireur (*m*) — *irregular soldier*

fusiller — *to shoot*

guerre-éclair (*f*)
'blitzkrieg', lightning war

harcèlement (*m*) — *harrying*

harceler — *to harry*

îlot (*m*) de résistance
pocket of resistance

s'implanter — *to establish itself*

interpellation (*f*) — *questioning*

jour (*m*) J — *D-day*

libérateur (*m*) — *liberator*

libération (*f*) — *liberation*

ligne (*f*) de démarcation
demarcation line

loyauté (*f*) — *loyalty*

maquis (*m*) — *the Resistance*

maquisard (*m*)
member of the Resistance

maréchal (*m*) — *marshal*

massacrer — *to massacre*

milice (*f*) — *militia*

mobilisation (*f*) — *mobilisation*

mouvement (*m*) — *movement*

narguer — *to flout*

otage (*m*) — *hostage*

papillon (*m*) — *sticker, bill*

parachuter — *to parachute*

paralyser	*to paralyse*	réfractaire (*m*)	*draft dodger*
patriote (*m/f*)	*patriot*	régime (*m*) de Vichy	*the Vichy régime*
pays (*m*) allié	*allied country*	renforcement (*m*)	*reinforcement*
percée (*f*)	*breakthrough*	représailles (*fpl*)	*reprisals*
piller	*to pillage*	réseau (*m*) d'évasion	*escape network*
poignée (*f*) d'hommes		résistant/e (*m/f*)	*resistance fighter*
	handful of men	revers (*m*)	*setback*
population (*f*) civile		riposte (*f*)	*counter-attack*
	civilian population	sabotage (*m*)	*sabotage*
presse (*f*) clandestine		saboter	*to sabotage*
	underground press	sévices (*mpl*)	*ill treatment*
prisonnier (*m*) de guerre		sol (*m*) français	*French soil*
	prisoner of war	tournant (*m*)	*turning point*
privations (*fpl*)	*hardship*	tract (*m*)	*pamphlet*
rafle (*f*)	*round-up*	trahison (*f*)	*betrayal*
rallier	*to unite*	traître (*m*)	*traitor*
rassembler	*to round up*	traquer	*to track down*
rationnement (*m*)	*rationing*	troupes (*fpl*)	*troops*
ravager#	*to lay waste*	vainqueur (*m*)	*victor*
ravitaillement (*m*)	*resupplying*	zone (*f*) occupée	*occupied zone*
recrue (*f*)	*recruit*		

exercer# des représailles contre	*to carry out reprisals against*
malgré des revers et des pertes considérables	*despite setbacks and heavy losses*
Moulin fut brutalisé par ses tortionnaires	*Moulin was brutally treated by his torturers*
porter un coup à la machine de guerre nazie	*to deal a blow to the nazi war machine*
prendre# l'ennemi à revers	*to attack the enemy from behind*
les autorités vichyssoises	*the Vichy authorities*
des attaques contre des objectifs allemands	*attacks on German targets*

le bilan des morts est aléatoire	*the death toll is unknown*
le rôle de la presse clandestine	*the role of the underground press*
la guerre psychologique	*the psychological war*
mourir# pour la patrie	*to die for one's country*
faire# un coup d'éclat	*to create a commotion*
faire# quelque chose en cachette	*to do something secretly*

LA FRANCOPHONIE

abâtardi/e	*bastardised*
accent (*m*)	*accent*
amalgame (*m*)	*mixture*
analphabète	*illiterate*
s'angliciser	*to become anglicised*
anglophone	*English-speaking*
autochtone	*native*
autonomie (*f*)	*self-determination*
bilingue	*bilingual*
bilinguisme (*m*)	*bilingualism*
chauvin/e	*chauvinistic*
coexistence (*f*)	*co-existence*
colonisation (*f*)	*colonisation*
Créole (*m*)	*Creole language*
de souche latine	*of Latin origin*
décolonisation (*f*)	*decolonisation*
dégénérescence (*f*)	*degeneration*
enraciné/e	*deep-rooted*
évoluer	*to evolve*
ex-colonies (*fpl*)	*former colonies*
s'exprimer	*to express oneself*
francophile (*m/f*)	*lover of France*

francophone	*French-speaking*
franglais (*m*)	*French/English mix*
hégémonie (*f*) culturelle	*cultural domination*
s'imposer	*to dominate*
langue (*f*) administrative	*administrative language*
langue (*f*) maternelle	*mother tongue*
langue (*f*) officielle	*official language*
langue (*f*) véhiculaire	*common language*
lien (*m*) historique	*historic link*
Métropole (*f*)	*France*
orbite (*f*) française	*French sphere of influence*
parlant (*m*) français	*French speaker*
patois (*m*)	*dialect*
périphrase (*f*)	*circumlocution*
pied-noir (*m*)	*Algerian-born French person*
puriste (*m/f*)	*purist*
rayonner	*to extend*
ressortissant/e (*m/f*)	*national*
supplanter	*to take the place of*

soumis/e à l'influence française	*under French influence*
avoir# quelque chose en commun avec	*to have something in common with*
le français du Québec a des spécificités	*Canadian French has some idiosyncracies*
sous dépendance française	*a French dependency*
des liens privilégiés avec le Maghreb	*preferential ties with North Africa*
les notices sont rédigées en deux langues	*notices are drawn up in two languages*
le français véhicule le dialogue	*French is the common language for conversation*
les anciennes colonies françaises et belges	*former French and Belgian colonies*
les DOM-TOM (Départements et territoires d'Outre-Mer)	*French overseas administrative regions and territories*
un journal d'expression française	*a French-language newspaper*
un sabir fait de français et d'arabe	*a mixture of French and Arabic*

LA POLITIQUE

abstentionnisme (*m*)	*abstaining*
affaires (*fpl*) étrangères	*foreign affairs*
aller# aux urnes	*to go to the polls*
alternance (*f*)	*handing over of power*
bourgeois/e	*middle-class*
briguer	*to canvass*
bureau (*m*) de vote	*polling station*
campagne (*f*)	*campaign*
chef (*m*) d'État	*head of state*
circonscription (*f*)	*constituency*
cohabiter	*to work together*
décideurs (*mpl*)	*decision-makers*
décréter#	*to order, decree*
délégué/e (*m/f*)	*delegate*
démentir#	*to deny*
démission (*f*)	*resignation*
député (*m*)	*MP*
désaccord (*m*)	*disagreement*
dictature (*f*)	*dictatorship*
discours (*m*)	*speech*
électeur/trice (*m/f*)	*constituent*
élection (*f*) cantonale	*local election*
élection (*f*) municipale	*municipal election*
élection (*f*) partielle	*by-election*
électorat (*m*)	*electorate*
élire#	*to elect*
élus (*mpl*)	*elected members*
engagement (*m*)	*commitment*
entretiens (*mpl*)	*talks*

gauchiste (*m*)	*left-winger*
hémicycle (*m*)	
benches in the National Assembly	
homologue (*m*)	
counterpart, opposite number	
jour (*m*) des élections	*polling day*
légiférer#	*to legislate*
majoritaire	*in the majority*
manifester	*to demonstrate*
membre (*m*) de la droite	*right-winger*
opposant (*m*)	*opponent*
parlementaire (*m/f*)	*MP*
partage (*m*) du pouvoir	*power sharing*
parti (*m*) au pouvoir	*party in office*
parti (*m*) conservateur	
Conservative party	
parti (*m*) travailliste	*Labour party*
politique (*f*)	*politics, policy*
politisé/e	*politically aware*

porte-parole (*m*)	*spokesperson*
pouvoir (*m*)	*power*
pouvoirs (*mpl*)	*public authorities*
préfet (*m*)	*prefect (local government)*
premier ministre (*m*)	*prime minister*
prolétaire	*working-class*
promesse (*f*)	*promise*
proportionnelle (*f*)	
proportional representation	
score (*m*)	*result*
scrutin (*m*)	*ballot*
septennat (*m*)	*seven-year term of office*
siéger#	*to sit*
sommet (*m*)	*summit*
sondage (*m*)	*opinion poll*
suffrage (*m*) universel	*votes for all*
voix (*f*)	*vote*
voter massivement	
to vote overwhelmingly	

la participation aux scrutins électoraux	*turnout at the polls*
lancer# un appel au gouvernement	*to appeal to the government*
suivre# des démarches pour	*to take steps to*
il incombe au gouvernement d'agir	*it's up to the government to act*
le scrutin majoritaire	*first past the post system*
politiquement correct	*politically correct*
faire# reculer les inégalités sociales	*to reduce unfairness in society*
sur le plan politique	*on a political level*
conserver son siège	*to keep his/her seat*
préconiser des mesures à long terme	*to be in favour of long-term measures*
se faire# plébisciter	*to gain a landslide victory*

LA GASTRONOMIE

additif (*m*)	*additive*
alimentation (*f*) de base	*staple diet*
alimenter	*to nourish*
aliments (*mpl*) complets	*wholefoods*
aliments (*mpl*) organiques	*wholefoods*
allégé/e	*low-fat*
appétit (*m*)	*appetite*
aromate (*m*)	*herb, spice*
aromatiser	*to flavour*
arôme (*m*)	*aroma*
artisanal/e	*locally produced*
assaisonnement (*m*)	*seasoning, dressing*
bénéfique	*beneficial*
biologique	*natural, organic*
bouchée (*f*)	*mouthful*
calorie (*f*)	*calorie*
cholestérol (*m*)	*cholesterol*
consommateur/trice (*m/f*)	*customer*
consommation (*f*)	*consumption, drink*
consommer	*to eat, consume*
couvert (*m*)	*place setting, cover charge*
crustacés (*mpl*)	*shellfish*
cuisine (*f*) du terroir	*local cooking*
culinaire	*culinary*
dégustation (*f*)	*tasting*
délice (*m*)	*delight*
désaltérer#	*to quench thirst*
épicé/e	*spicy*
féculents (*mpl*)	*starchy foods*

friandise (*f*)	*delicacy*
gastronome (*m/f*)	*gourmet*
gastronomique	*gourmet*
gorgée (*f*)	*mouthful*
se gorger# de	*to gorge oneself on*
goûteux/euse	*tasty*
haute cuisine (*f*)	*top-class cooking*
ingérer#	*to eat, to ingest*
ingrédient (*m*)	*ingredient*
intoxication (*f*) alimentaire	*food poisoning*
ligne (*f*)	*figure*
matière (*f*) grasse	*fat content*
millésime (*m*)	*vintage*
mousseux/euse	*sparkling*
odorat (*m*)	*sense of smell*
œnologie (*f*)	*science of winemaking*
pièce (*f*) de résistance	*main dish*
plat (*m*) de résistance	*main dish of the meal*
plat (*m*) du jour	*dish of the day, today's special*
plateau (*m*) de fromages	*cheese board*
plats (*mpl*) cuisinés	*ready-cooked dishes*
priser	*to prize, appreciate*
produit (*m*) laitier	*dairy product*
recette (*f*)	*recipe*
rendement (*m*)	*yield*
repas (*m*) d'affaires	*business lunch*
restaurant (*m*) diététique	*health-food restaurant*

restaurant (*m*) gastronomique		savoureux/euse	*tasty*
	gourmet restaurant	valeur (*f*) nutritive	*nutritional value*
restaurateur (*m*)	*restaurant owner*	végétarien/ne	*vegetarian*
restauration (*f*) rapide	*fast food*	vignoble (*m*)	*vineyard*
récolte (*f*)	*harvest*		

manger# sur le pouce	*to snack*
le savoir vivre	*an appreciation of how to live well*
la restauration rapide	*fast-food industry*
avoir# une prédilection pour	*to be partial to*
privilégier la cuisine traditionnelle	*to prefer traditional cooking*
manger# plus sainement	*to eat more healthily*
l'équipement électroménager	*domestic appliances*
les plats préparés surgelés	*ready-made frozen foods*
avoir# une alimentation équilibrée	*to eat a balanced diet*
riche/pauvre en calories	*with a high/low calorie content*
l'appétit vient en mangeant	*eating whets your appetite*
aimer les plaisirs de la table	*to like one's food*
se mettre# au régime	*to go on a diet*
quelle est la composition du gâteau?	*what's the cake made of?*
c'est le seul art qui parle aux cinq sens	*it's the only art that appeals to all five senses*

ADRESSES UTILES

Banque d'information politique, 8 avenue de l'Opéra, 75001 Paris

Centre d'information civique, 242 bis boulevard Saint Germain, 75007 Paris

Parti Communiste Français, 2 place du Colonel Fabien, 75940 Paris

Front National, 8 rue du Général-Clergerie, 75116 Paris

Parti Socialiste, 10 rue Solférino, 75333 Paris

U.D.F. 42 boulevard Latour-Maubourg, 75007 Paris

R.P.R. 123 rue de Lille, 75007 Paris

French Tourist Office, 178 Piccadilly, London W1V 0AL

Bureau pour l'enseignement de la langue et de la civilisation française à l'étranger, 9 rue Llomaud, 75005 Paris

La Maison de France, 8 avenue de l'Opéra, 75001 Paris

Université du vin, château de Suze, 26790 Suze la Brousse, France

Le Cordon Bleu École de Cuisine, 8 rue Léon Delhomme, 75015 Paris

SOPEXA, 43-45 rue de Naples, 75008 Paris (food and agricultural products)

CONSEIL DE VOCABULAIRE

Rappel – Pour bien apprendre du vocabulaire, il faut faire quelque chose d'actif. C'est en forgeant qu'on devient forgeron!

Pour bien apprendre des mots, c'est une bonne idée de les classer par catégories. Ce livre les a classés sous des thèmes, et par ordre alphabétique. Copiez les mots et les phrases sous des classements différents. Par exemple:

Dans la politique, on pourrait regrouper tous les verbes, et dans une autre liste tous les adjectifs:

Verbe	Adjectif	
briguer	majoritaire	
conserver	politisé	
voter	public,	etc.

Pour une région de la France, il y a les aspects positifs et négatifs:

Positif	Négatif	
carnaval	arriéré	
dynamisme	faiblesse	
doté de	démuni,	etc.

LES GENS

LA FAMILLE

adoptif/ve	*adopted*
adultère (*m*)	*adultery*
âge (*m*) de consentement	
	age of consent
agence (*f*) matrimoniale	
	dating agency
allocation (*f*) familiale	*child benefit*
cellule (*f*) familiale	*family unit*
cohabitation (*f*)	*living together*
cohabiter	*to live together*
concubinage (*m*)	
	common-law marriage
conflit (*m*) conjugal	*marital strife*
conjoint/e (*m/f*)	*spouse*
se désagréger#	*to break up*
épouser	*to get married*
esprit (*m*) de famille	*family feeling*
famille (*f*) adoptive	*foster home*
famille (*f*) monoparentale	
	single-parent family
famille (*f*) nombreuse	*large family*
famille (*f*) nucléaire	*nuclear family*
femme (*f*) battue	*battered wife*

fonder un foyer (*m*)	*to set up a home*
foyer (*m*) brisé	*broken home*
homme (*m*) au foyer	*house husband*
liens (*m*) familiaux	*family ties*
majeur/e	*over 18*
mariage (*m*)	*marriage*
se marier	*to get married*
ménagère (*f*)	*housewife*
mère (*f*) d'accueil	*surrogate mother*
mineur/e	*under age*
mœurs (*fpl*)	*morals*
monogame	*monogamous*
natalité (*f*)	*birth rate*
nid (*m*) douillet	*cosy nest*
partenaire (*m/f*)	*partner*
planning (*m*) familial	*family planning*
rapports (*mpl*) sexuels	
	sexual intercourse
structure (*f*) familiale	
	family structure
s'unir	*to be joined in marriage*
veuf/veuve (*m/f*)	*widower/widow*
vie (*f*) affective	*emotional life*
vie (*f*) en couple	*life together*

contrat m de mariage	*marriage contract*
se mettre# en ménage	*to set up house together*
vivre# en union libre	*to live together*
se solder par un divorce	*to end in divorce*

la garde des enfants · *custody of the children*

le taux de nuptialité est en baisse · *the marriage rate is in decline*

vivre# en dehors du cadre de mariage · *to live outside the framework of marriage*

les naissances hors mariage · *births outside marriage*

LE FÉMINISME

abaisser · *to humiliate*

ambitieux/euse · *ambitious*

améliorer · *to improve*

autonome · *self-sufficient*

carrière (*f*) · *career*

condition (*f*) féminine · *woman's lot*

contradictoire · *contradictory*

se culpabiliser · *to feel guilty*

se débrouiller · *to cope*

désapprouver quelque chose · *to disapprove of something*

discrimination (*f*) sexuelle · *sexual discrimination*

droits (*mpl*) de la femme · *women's rights*

égalitaire · *egalitarian*

égalité (*f*) des chances · *equality of opportunity*

égalité (*f*) des sexes · *equality of the sexes*

émancipation (*f*) · *emancipation*

émancipé/e · *liberated*

s'épanouir · *to be fulfilled*

grief (*m*) · *grievance*

groupe (*m*) féministe · *women's group*

harcèlement (*m*) sexuel · *sexual harassment*

idéaliser · *to idealise*

interdit (*m*) · *taboo*

libération (*f*) de la femme · *women's liberation*

liberté (*f*) · *freedom*

mal vu/e · *poorly thought of*

maternel/le · *motherly*

maternité (*f*) · *motherhood*

mère (*f*) célibataire · *unmarried mother*

militantisme (*m*) · *militancy*

misogynie (*f*) · *misogyny*

mouvement (*m*) féministe · *feminist movement*

moyens (*mpl*) financiers · *financial means*

objet (*m*) érotique · *sex object*

phallocrate (*m*) · *male chauvinist*

pionnière (*f*) · *pioneer*

préjugé (*m*) · *prejudice*

pressions (*fpl*) sociales · *social pressures*

réclamer · *to demand*

répartition (f) des rôles	*division of the roles*
rester au foyer	*to stay at home*
sexe (m) opposé	*opposite sex*

sexisme (m)	*sexism*
stéréotype (m)	*stereotype*
subir	*to be subjected to*
surmonter	*to overcome*

à travail égal, salaire égal	*equal pay for equal work*
être# conditionné/e à	*to be conditioned to*
s'intéresser avant tout à sa carrière	*to be a career person*
le partage des tâches ménagères	*sharing the household jobs*
l'avortement sur demande	*abortion on demand*
la moitié de la race humaine	*half of the human race*
accéder# à la vie professionnelle	*to have access to a career*
conserver son nom de jeune fille	*to keep her maiden name*
être# déterminée par sa fonction de procréation	*to be bound by their reproductive function*
démythifier la maternité	*to remove the myths about motherhood*
rémunérer les femmes au foyer	*to pay housewives for their work*
se sentir# prisonnier/ière	*to feel trapped*
servir# de modèle à émuler	*to act as a role model*

LE CONFLIT DES GÉNÉRATIONS

agaçant/e	*annoying*
autonomie (f)	*self-sufficiency*
autoritaire	*authoritarian*
autorité (f) parentale	*parental authority*
bouder	*to sulk*
comportement (m)	*behaviour*

se comporter	*to behave*
confiance (f)	*confidence*
contredire#	*to contradict*
coup (m) de cafard	*fit of depression*
crise (f)	*crisis*
culture (f) adolescente	*teenage culture*
délaisser	*to neglect*
dépassé/e	*old-fashioned*
désaccord (m)	*disagreement*

désobéir à quelqu'un
to disobey someone

dialoguer avec *to communicate with*

dispute (*f*) *argument*

environnement (*m*) stable
stable environment

échelle (*f*) des valeurs *scale of values*

élever *to rear, raise*

étouffant/e *suffocating*

excès (*m*) d'autorité *over-strictness*

faire# une fugue *to run away*

fermeté (*f*) *firmness*

frictions (*f*) parents-enfants
parent-child conflicts

hostilité (*f*) *hostility*

incompréhension (*f*)
lack of understanding

indulgent/e *lenient*

liens (*mpl*) familiaux *family ties*

lubie (*f*) *whim, fad*

marginal (*m*) *drop-out*

mépriser *to scorn*

mûr/e *mature*

s'occuper des enfants
to look after the children

ouverture (*f*) *openness*

progéniture (*f*) *offspring*

protecteur/trice à l'excès
over-protective

rapports (*mpl*) *relationships*

rebelle (*m/f*) *rebel*

se rebeller contre *to rebel against*

rechigner *to look sour*

reproche (*m*) *criticism*

respecter *to respect*

se révolter *to rebel*

sentiment (*m*) *feeling*

se sentir# brimé/e *to feel got at*

se sentir# incompris/e
to feel misunderstood

sévère *strict*

soucis (*m*) *care, worry*

soutenir# *to support*

uni/e *united*

valeurs (*fpl*) familiales *family values*

les jeunes désœuvrés
young people with nothing to do

rompre avec son enfance
to break with one's childhood

être# ballotté/e entre des sentiments contraires
to be torn between conflicting emotions

la convention internationale des droits de l'enfant
the international convention on children's rights

la transmission des valeurs traditionnelles
the passing on of traditional values

accorder de l'autonomie à
to grant someone their independence

manquer de respect envers
to lack respect for

s'enfermer dans la chambre
to shut oneself away in the bedroom

40

mener# à l'harmonie familiale	*to make for family harmony*
être# replié/e sur soi-même	*to be inward-looking*
imposer leur volonté	*to impose their will*
mes parents dramatisent trop	*my parents over-react*

LES GENS CÉLÈBRES

admirer	*to admire*
anonymat (*m*)	*anonymity*
bain (*m*) de foule	*walkabout*
blasé/e	*laid-back*
célébrité (*f*)	*fame*
couronne (*f*)	*crown*
culte (*m*) du héros	*hero-worship*
de renommée mondiale	*world-famous*
devoir (*m*)	*duty*
doué/e	*talented*
dynastie (*f*)	*dynasty*
extravagant/e	*flamboyant*
héritier (*m*) de la couronne	
	heir apparent
hors d'atteinte	*beyond reach*
s'identifier à	*to identify with*
idolâtrer	*to idolise*
impressionnant/e	*impressive*
inaugurer	*to unveil, open*

influencer#	*to influence*
inspirant/e	*inspiring*
luxe (*m*)	*luxury*
millionnaire (*m/f*)	*millionaire*
mode (*m*) de vie	*life-style*
monarchie (*f*)	*monarchy*
notoire	*notorious*
personnalité (*f*)	*famous person*
popularité (*f*)	*popularity*
privilégié/e	*privileged*
régner#	*to reign*
reine (*f*)	*queen*
remarquable	*remarkable*
renommé/e pour	
	renowned for, famous for
richesse (*f*)	*wealth*
roi (*m*)	*king*
snobisme (*m*)	*snobbery*
souverain/e (*m/f*)	*sovereign*
vedette (*f*)	*star*
vivats (*mpl*)	*cheers*

une légende de son vivant	*a legend in his/her own lifetime*
mener# une vie intolérable	*to lead an unbearable life*
bénéficier de son parrainage	*to benefit from her patronage*
présider une cérémonie	*to be guest of honour at a ceremony*

41

la famille royale britannique	*the British royal family*
exercer une fascination sur	*to exert a fascination over*
rendre# hommage à	*to pay tribute to*
très populaire auprès des jeunes	*very popular amongst young people*
il ne peut pas passer inaperçu	*he cannot go unrecognised*

ADRESSES UTILES

Centre d'information jeunesse, CIJ Seine et Marne, 36 avenue de la Libération, 77000 Melun

Centre d'information et de documentation jeunesse, 101 quai Branly, 75740 Paris

Centre national d'Information et de documentation des femmes et familles, 7 rue du Jura, 75013 Paris

Centre d'information civique, 242 bis boulevard Saint-Germain, 75006 Paris

Centre d'orientation, de documentation et d'Information féminine, 81 rue Sénac, 13001 Marseille

Agence Femmes Information, 9 cité Trévise, 75009 Paris

Centre européen de la jeunesse, 30 rue Pierre de Coubertin, 67000 Strasbourg

Conseil national des associations de jeunesse et d'éducation populaire, 15 rue Martel, 75010 Paris

CONSEIL DE VOCABULAIRE

Rappel – Pour bien apprendre du vocabulaire, il faut faire quelque chose d'actif. C'est en forgeant qu'on devient forgeron!

Qu'est-ce qui va ensemble? Choisissez un nombre raisonnable de nouveaux mots (mettons 20) et écrivez-les sur de petits bouts de papier.

Par exemple:

  marginal   *mûr*   *bouder etc.*

En même temps, écrivez les mêmes mots en anglais sur d'autres bouts de papier:

  drop-out   *mature*   *to sulk*

Puis, vous mélangez les bouts de papier et vous essayez de trouver les mots qui vont ensemble. Refaites l'exercice quelques jours plus tard.

Si vous trouvez certains mots difficiles à retenir, collez-les avec du 'Blu-Tack' côte à côte français-anglais dans un endroit où vous allez souvent chaque jour (par exemple dans la salle de bains, près de votre lit). Quand vous pensez les avoir appris, vous retournez les cartes avec le français au mur, et vous vous donnez une petite interrogation chaque fois que vous revoyez les mots au mur.

L'INFORMATIQUE

LES ORDINATEURS

annuaire (*m*)	*directory*
base (*f*) de données	*database*
brancher	*to connect up*
clavier (*m*)	*keyboard*
clavier tactile (*m*)	*concept keyboard*
code (*m*) d'accès	*password*
compatible	*compatible*
convivial/e	*user-friendly*
copie (*f*) pirate	*pirate copy*
disque (*m*) compact-ROM	*CD-Rom*
disque (*m*) dur	*hard disk*
disque (*m*) souple	*floppy disk*
disquette (*f*)	*floppy disk*
écran (*m*)	*screen*
effraction (*f*) informatique	*hacking*
fiable	*reliable*
fichier (*m*)	*file*
imprimante (*f*)	*printer*
infographie (*f*)	*computer graphics*
informatiser	*to computerise*
jargon (*m*) informatique	*computerese*
jeu (*m*) électronique	*computer game*
listage (*m*)	*printout*
logiciel (*m*)	*software*
machine (*f*) de traitement de texte	*word processor*

matériel (*m*)	*hardware*
messageries (*fpl*) électroniques	*electronic bulletin board*
médiathèque (*f*)	*multi-media reference library*
mémoire (*f*)	*memory*
Minitel (*m*)	*home telecommunications terminal*
miniteler	*to contact someone via Minitel*
minitéliste (*m/f*)	*Minitel user*
ordinateur (*m*) individuel	*PC*
portatif/ve	*portable*
progiciel (*m*)	*software package*
puce (*f*)	*microchip*
réalité (*f*) virtuelle	*virtual reality*
réseau (*m*)	*network*
service (*m*) bancaire	*banking service*
souris (*f*)	*mouse*
terminal (*m*)	*terminal*
tomber en panne	*to crash*
touche (*f*)	*key*
traitement (*m*) graphique	*graphics*
utilisateur/trice (*m/f*)	*user*
virus (*m*)	*virus*

l'ère de l'informatique	*the computer age*
la sécurité des informations	*data security*
la loi informatique et libertés	*data protection act*
la qualité d'entrée égale la qualité de sortie	*garbage in, garbage out*
traiter quelque chose informatiquement	*to process something on a computer*
entrer dans le système	*to log on*
sortir du système	*to log off*
un minitéliste dialogue en direct avec	*a Minitel user interacts directly with*
Le Minitel est une spécificité française	*Minitel is unique to France*
faire# les courses par l'intermédiaire du Minitel	*to shop using Minitel*
initié/e à l'informatique	*computer literate*
l'enseignement assisté par ordinateur	*computer-assisted learning*

ADRESSES UTILES

France Télécom, 6 place d'Alleray, 75015 Paris

Association française des utilisateurs de téléphones et de télécommunications, B.P.1, 92430 Marnes-La-Coquette

INTELMATIQUE, 175 rue du Chevaleret, 75646 Paris

Service Télétel, 36 rue du Commandant Mouchotte, 75675 Paris

CONSEIL DE VOCABULAIRE

Rappel – Pour bien apprendre du vocabulaire, il faut faire quelque chose d'actif. C'est en forgeant qu'on devient forgeron!

Travaillez avec quelques partenaires. Choisissez des lettres au hasard et essayez de trouver un verbe, un adjectif et un nom qui commencent avec cette lettre et qui sont associés à ce thème.

Par exemple: P

verbe: protéger   adjectif: pratique   nom: progiciel

On peut voir qui est le premier à trouver les solutions!

LES MÉDIAS

LA TÉLÉVISION

actualité (f) scénarisée
'faction', drama documentary

allumer — to switch on

annonce (f) — announcement

annonceur/annonceuse (m/f)
announcer

antenne (f) parabolique — satellite dish

caméra (f) — video camera

canal (m) — channel

chaîne (f) — channel

chaîne (f) cryptée
subscription channel

couverture (f) intensive
blanket coverage

décodeur (m) — decoder

diffuser — to broadcast

divertissant/e — entertaining

documentaire (m) — documentary

documentaire (m) animalier
wildlife documentary

documentaire (m) touristique
travel programme

doublé/e — dubbed

droits (mpl) d'antenne
television rights

émetteur (m) — transmitter

émission (f) — broadcast

émission (f) scolaire
schools programme

émission (f) sportive
sports programme

en différé — recorded, replay

en direct — live

en noir et blanc — black and white

équipe (f) de tournage — camera crew

flash (m) d'information — newsflash

flash (m) publicitaire
television commercial

génériques (mpl) — credits

grille (f) des programmes — schedule

heure (f) d'émission — broadcast time

heures (fpl) de grande écoute
peak viewing

image (f) défectueuse — poor picture

interruption (f) — interruption

local/e — local

long métrage (m) — feature film

magnétoscope (m) — video recorder

moyen (m) d'évasion — form of escape

nullité (f) — flop

numérique — digital

passer sur l'antenne — to go on the air

perturbation (f) — disturbance

primé/e — award-winning

programmation (f) — programming

programme (m) bas de gamme
downmarket programme

programme (*m*) haut de gamme
upmarket programme

public-cible (*m*) *target audience*

qualité (*f*) de l'image *picture quality*

questions (*fpl*) d'actualité
current affairs

réalisation (*f*) *production*

réception (*f*) *reception*

recevoir# *to receive*

redevance (*f*) *licence*

rediffusion (*f*) *repeat*

régional/e *local*

reprise (*f*) *repeat*

réseau (*m*) *network*

société (*f*) de télévision
television company

speaker/speakerine (*m/f*) *announcer*

super-production (*f*) *blockbuster*

taux (*m*) d'écoute *viewing figures*

télé-poubelle (*f*)
trash-television, rubbish

téléachat (*m*) *TV shopping*

télécommande (*f*) *remote control*

téléspectateur/trice (*m/f*) *viewer*

télétexte (*m*) *Teletext*

télévision (*f*) du matin
breakfast television

télévision (*f*) en couleurs
colour television

télévision (*f*) par câble
cable television

télévision (*f*) par satellite
satellite television

transmettre# *to transmit*

valeur (*f*) éducative
educational value

vidéocassette (*f*) à caractère
pornographique
pornographic video nasty

vidéocassette (*f*) à caractère violent
video nasty

village (*m*) global *global village*

zapper *to channel-hop*

zapping (*m*) *channel-hopping*

---

la banalisation de la violence *making violence a commonplace event*

changer# de chaîne *to change channels*

faire# de la publicité à la télévision *to advertise on television*

la course à l'audience *competition for viewers*

parler en utilisant des phrases toutes faites *to talk in sound-bites*

une fenêtre ouverte sur le monde *an open window on the world*

regarder l'histoire en train de se faire *to watch history in the making*

sous-titré/e pour les mal-entendants *subtitled for the hard of hearing*

rester cloué/e devant la télévision *to sit glued in front of the television*

diffusé/e en direct dans le salon	*beamed straight into the living room*
un/e envoyé/e permanent/e à l'étranger	*foreign correspondent*
notre envoyé/e spécial/e	*our special correspondent*

LA RADIO

auditeur/auditrice (*m/f*)	*listener*
audition (*f*)	*reception*
bande (*f*) de fréquences	*waveband*
brancher sur	*to tune into*
capter	*to pick up*
disc-jockey (*m*)	*disc-jockey*
fond (*m*) sonore	*background noise*
fréquence (*f*)	*frequency*
indicatif (*m*)	*signature tune*
interviewer (*m*)	*interviewer*
intervieweuse (*f*)	*interviewer*
longueur (*f*) d'ondes	*wavelength*

personnalité (*f*) de la radio	*broadcaster*
pièce (*f*) radiophonique	*radio play*
présentateur/présentatrice (*m/f*)	*presenter*
radio (*f*) libre	*commercial radio station*
radiodiffusion (*f*)	*broadcasting*
reportage (*m*)	*report*
son (*m*)	*sound*
station (*f*) de radio	*radio station*
stéréo (*f*)	*stereo*
sur grandes ondes	*on long wave*

vous êtes à l'écoute de France-Inter	*you are listening to France-Inter*
c'est Jean Lebrun au micro	*the presenter is Jean Lebrun*
écouter une émission en modulation de fréquence	*to listen to a VHF/FM broadcast*

LA PRESSE

abonnement (*m*)	*subscription*
abonné/e (*m/f*)	*subscriber*
agence (*f*) de presse	*press agency*
annonce (*f*)	*announcement*
article (*m*)	*article*
article (*m*) de tête	*leader, editorial*
chroniqueur/euse (*m/f*)	*columnist*

collaborateur/trice (*m/f*)	*contributor*
communiqué (*m*) de presse	*press release*
conférence (*f*) de presse	*press conference*
droit (*m*) d'auteur	*copyright*
coquille (*f*)	*misprint*
courrier (*m*) du cœur	*agony column*
de caractère (*m*) diffamatoire	*libellous*

diffamation (*f*)	*libel*
divertir	*to amuse*
éditeur/trice (*m/f*)	*publisher*
enquête (*f*)	*investigation*
envoyé/e (*m/f*) spécial/e	*special correspondent*
équipe (*f*) de rédaction	*editorial team*
exemplaire (*m*)	*copy*
faits divers (*mpl*)	*news in brief*
grand public (*m*)	*the general public*
hebdomadaire (*m*)	*weekly (also adj)*
illustré (*m*)	*magazine*
imprimer	*to print*
journal (*m*) du dimanche	*Sunday newspaper*
journal (*m*) plein format	*broadsheet*
journal (*m*) sérieux	*quality newspaper*
journalisme (*m*) d'enquête	*investigative journalism*
la une (*f*)	*front page*
le gros titre (*m*)	*headline*
liberté (*f*) de la presse	*freedom of the press*
mensuel/le	*monthly*
mise (*f*) en page	*layout*

nombre (*m*) de lecteurs	*readership*
objectif/ve	*objective*
petites annonces (*fpl*)	*small ads*
pigiste (*m/f*)	*freelance journalist*
prix (*m*) de revient	*cost price*
publier	*to publish*
quotidien (*m*) populaire	*tabloid daily*
rédacteur/trice (*m/f*)	*editor*
reportage (*m*)	*report*
reportage (*m*) exclusif	*an exclusive*
revue (*f*) de luxe	*glossy magazine*
revue (*f*) professionnelle	*trade magazine*
rubrique (*f*)	*section*
rubrique (*f*) affaires	*business section*
rubrique (*f*) des spectacles	*entertainments column*
rubrique (*f*) sportive	*sports pages*
supplément (*m*)	*supplement*
supplément (*m*) en couleurs	*colour supplement*
téléscripteur (*m*)	*teleprinter*
tirage (*m*)	*circulation*
zone (*f*) de diffusion	*circulation area*

souscrire# un abonnement à	*to take out a subscription to*
tenir# le lecteur au courant	*to keep the reader informed*
garantir la libre parole	*to guarantee free speech*
faire# les gros titres	*to make the headlines*
la presse à sensation	*the gutter press*

essayer# de museler la presse — *to try to muzzle the press*

un journal à grand tirage — *mass circulation newspaper*

s'ingérer# dans la vie privée de quelqu'un — *to intrude on somebody's privacy*

LA PUBLICITÉ

acheteur/euse (*m/f*) — *buyer*

agence (*f*) de publicité — *advertising agency*

annonce (*f*) — *advertisement*

campagne (*f*) promotionnelle — *advertising campaign*

campagne (*f*) publicitaire — *advertising campaign*

client/e (*m/f*) — *customer*

clientèle (*f*) — *the customers*

concurrence (*f*) — *competition*

déformer la réalité — *to distort the truth*

échantillon (*m*) gratuit — *free sample*

efficace — *effective*

embarras (*m*) du choix — *too much choice*

évoquer — *to evoke, to conjure up*

exagération (*f*) — *exaggeration*

exploité/e — *exploited*

faire# appel à — *to appeal to*

image (*f*) de marque — *brand image*

informatif/ve — *informative*

insidieux/euse — *insidious, underhand*

invraisemblable — *unlikely, implausible*

journal (*m*) gratuit — *free paper*

lettre (*f*) personnalisée — *mail-shot*

marque (*f*) — *make, brand*

mensongère — *deceitful*

mentir# — *to lie*

normes (*fpl*) publicitaires — *advertising standards*

panneau (*m*) d'affichage — *billboard*

partial/e — *prejudiced*

publicitaires (*m/fpl*) — *advertising executives*

publicité (*f*) cinématographique — *cinema advertising*

publicité (*f*) radiodiffusée — *radio advertising*

publicité (*f*) télévisuelle — *TV advertising*

réclame (*f*) — *advertisement*

ritournelle (*f*) publicitaire — *jingle*

slogan (*m*) — *slogan*

snobisme (*m*) — *snobbery*

spot (*m*) publicitaire — *commercial break*

usage (*m*) de l'érotisme — *use of sex*

ventes (*fpl*) accrues — *increased sales*

tenir# compte des réalités	*to take into account the facts*
exploiter le sexe	*to exploit sex*
un produit de consommation courante	*an everyday item*
se laisser manipuler par	*to let oneself be manipulated by*
pour ne pas être# en reste avec les voisins	*to keep up with the Jones's*
au-delà des moyens de	*beyond the (financial) means of*
une incitation à consommer	*an encouragement to consumption*
une société de consommation	*a consumer society*
inciter à dépenser de l'argent	*to encourage you to spend your money*
agir sur le subconscient	*to act on the subconscious*
faire# appel à nos instincts primitifs	*to appeal to our base instincts*
le lavage de cerveau	*brainwashing*

DIVERS

bienfaits (*mpl*)	*the benefits*
censure (*f*)	*censorship*
compréhension (*f*)	*understanding*
conscience (*f*) de	*awareness of*
crénau (*m*)	*niche*
diffuser	*to broadcast, disseminate*
l'écrit (*m*)	*the written word*
s'exprimer	*to express oneself*

influencer#	*to influence*
instruire#	*to educate*
liberté (*f*) d'information	*freedom of information*
les mass médias (*mpl*)	*the mass media*
nocif/ve	*harmful*
nuisible	*harmful*
pornographique	*pornographic*
propagande (*f*)	*propaganda*

un code de bonne conduite	*a code of good conduct*
la mise en orbite de	*the launch of (a product, magazine, etc.)*
le scandale est un thème vendeur	*scandal boosts sales*
obtenir# une bonne couverture médiatique	*to get good media coverage*
un événement médiatique	*a media event*

un homme informé en vaut deux	*forewarned is forearmed (Proverb)*
selon des sources bien informées	*according to well-informed sources*
l'opium du peuple	*the opium of the people*
agir sous la pression commerciale	*to act under commercial pressure*
les publications pour les jeunes	*teenage publications*

ADRESSES UTILES

France 2, 22 avenue Montaigne, 75387 Paris

TF1, 56 rue de l'Arrivée, 75015 Paris

France 3, 116 avenue du Président Kennedy, 75790 Paris

Conseil supérieur de l'audiovisuel, 56 rue Jacob, 75006 Paris

Radio France, 116 avenue du Président Kennedy, 75790 Paris

Institut de recherche et d'études publicitaires, 62 rue la Boétie, 75008 Paris

Centre d'étude des supports de presse, 32 avenue Georges-Mandel, 75016 Paris

Fédération internationale des journalistes, International Press Centre, Boulevard Charlemagne, 1 bte 5 B-1041 Bruxelles, Belgium

Bayard Presse Jeune (*Phosphore, Okapi*), 3–5 rue Bayard, 75008 Paris

CONSEIL DE VOCABULAIRE

Rappel – Pour bien apprendre du vocabulaire, il faut faire quelque chose d'actif. C'est en forgeant qu'on devient forgeron!

Vous faites une liste de mots à apprendre mais vous supprimez une lettre dans chaque mot. Par exemple, dans ce livre vous lisez:

un auditeur, un indicatif, le reportage, capter.

Vous écrivez une liste comme celle-ci:

un a_diteur = listener

un _ndicatif = signature tune

le reporta_e = report

cap_er = to pick up

Quelques jours plus tard vous regardez encore une fois votre liste. Pouvez-vous toujours remplir les lettres qui manquent?

— LE MONDE DU TRAVAIL —

LA CHASSE À L'EMPLOI

bureau (*m*) de placement
personnel agency

candidat/e (*m/f*) *applicant*

candidature (*f*) *application*

carrière (*f*) *career*

centre (*m*) d'orientation *careers office*

chasseur (*m*) de tête *headhunter*

contrat (*m*) *contract*

curriculum (*m*) vitae *curriculum vitae*

cursus (*m*) *career path*

débouché (*m*) *job opening*

demande (*f*) d'emploi *application*

demandeur/euse (*m/f*) d'emploi
job-hunter

diplômé/e *qualified*

entretien (*m*) *interview*

entrevue (*f*) *interview*

intérimaire *temporary*

lacune (*f*) *gap*

lettre (*f*) explicative *covering letter*

offre (*f*) d'emploi *job offer*

parcours (*m*) professionnel
professional career

poste (*m*) *post, position*

postulant/e (*m/f*) *applicant*

profil (*m*) du poste *job description*

recruter *to recruit*

recyclage (*m*) *retraining*

se recycler *to retrain*

référence (*f*) *reference*

refus (*m*) *rejection*

rejet (*m*) *rejection*

service (*m*) du personnel
personnel department

visite (*f*) impromptue *cold call*

un employeur qui ne fait pas de discrimination	*an equal opportunities employer*
les possibilités d'avancement	*career prospects*
un formulaire de demande d'emploi	*job application form*
fournir des références	*to act as a referee*
convoquer quelqu'un pour une entrevue	*to invite someone for an interview*
postuler pour un emploi	*to apply for a job*
poser sa candidature	*to submit one's application*
les conditions de travail	*conditions of employment*
conseiller/ère d'orientation professionnelle	*careers adviser*
exercer# une profession	*to carry out/practise a profession*

AU BUREAU

à l'appareil	on the line (phone)
base (f) de données	database
bureautique (f)	office automation
classeur (m)	filing cabinet
col (m) blanc	white-collar worker
communication (f) interurbaine	long-distance call
communication pour l'étranger	international call
coup (m) de téléphone	phone call
courrier (m) électronique	E-mail
dossier (m)	file
envoyer par télécopie	to fax (something)
envoyer une télécopie à	to fax (someone)
indicatif (m)	dialling code
machine (f) à écrire	typewriter
machine (f) de traitement de texte	word processor
ordinateur (m) de bureau	desktop computer
ordinateur (m) portatif	laptop
ordre (m) du jour	agenda
par téléphone	by telephone
passer	to put through (on phone)
photocopieur/copieuse (m/f)	photocopier
poste (m)	extension
raccrocher	to hang up (phone)
rappeler#	to call back (phone)
renseignements (mpl)	Directory Enquiries
répondeur (m) automatique	answerphone
standard (m)	switchboard
télé-travail (m)	teleworking
télécopie (f)	fax (message)
télécopieur (m)	fax machine
téléphone (m) cellulaire	cellular phone
téléphone (m) portatif	mobile phone
ticket (m)	luncheon voucher
travail (m) administratif	paperwork

le travail à plein temps n'est plus la norme	full-time working is no longer the norm
toucher 3000f par mois	to be paid 3000 francs a month
la ligne est occupée	the line's engaged
ne quittez pas	hold the line
vous êtes en ligne	you're through (on phone)
téléphoner à l'extérieur	to make an outside call
appeler# par l'automatique	to dial direct
faire# un faux numéro	to dial a wrong number
avoir# des heures de bureau	to work office hours

AU TRAVAIL

année (f) sabbatique	sabbatical year
avancement (m)	promotion
avantage (m) annexe	fringe benefit
boulot (m)	work
bulletin (m) de paie	payslip
bureaucratie (f)	bureaucracy
caisse (f) de retraite	pension scheme
collaboration (f)	teamwork
congé (m) de maternité	maternity leave
congé (m) de paternité	paternity leave
crèche (f)	crèche
départ (m) volontaire	voluntary redundancy
employer	to employ
feuille (f) de paie	payslip
frais (mpl) de voyage	travel expenses
heures (fpl) supplémentaires	overtime
horaire (m) variable	flexi-time
indépendant/e	self-employed
jour (m) férié	bank holiday
licenciement (m)	compulsory redundancy

métier (m)	trade, profession
partage (m) de poste	job-sharing
période (f) probatoire	probationary period
petit bénéfice (m)	perk
préretraite (f)	early retirement
rémunération (f)	payment
rendez-vous (m)	appointment
responsabilité (f)	responsibility
réunion (f)	meeting
salarié/e (m/f)	wage-earner
service (m)	department
syndicaliste (m/f)	trade union member
syndicat (m)	trade union
tâche (f)	task
traitement (m)	salary
travail (m) à mi-temps	part-time work
travail (m) à plein temps	full-time work
travail (m) au noir	moonlighting
travail (m) en équipe	shiftwork
voiture (f) de fonction	company car
voyage (m) d'affaires	business trip

faire# des affaires avec quelqu'un	to do business with someone
la sécurité de l'emploi	job security
la satisfaction au travail	job satisfaction
la formation sur le tas	on-the-job training
travailler à son propre compte	to be self-employed
donner son congé	to hand in your notice
travailler à domicile	to work from home
partir# en préretraite	to take early retirement
la CGT (Confédération générale du travail)	main French trade union

LES EMPLOYÉS

administratifs (*mpl*)	*admin staff*
apprenti/e (*m/f*)	*apprentice*
associé/e (*m/f*)	*partner*
cadre (*m/f*)	*executive*
chef (*m*) d'entreprise	*head of a company*
clientèle (*f*)	*customers*
collègue (*m/f*)	*colleague*
direction (*f*)	*management*
effectifs (*mpl*)	*workforce*
employé/e (*m/f*)	*employee*
employeur/euse (*m/f*)	*employer*
expert-conseil (*m*)	*consultant*
fabricant/e (*m/f*)	*manufacturer*
femme (*f*) d'affaires	*businesswoman*

fonctionnaire (*m/f*)	*civil servant*
fournisseur (*m*)	*supplier*
gérant/e (*m/f*)	*manager/ess*
gestion (*f*)	*management*
homme (*m*) d'affaires	*businessman*
main (*f*) d'œuvre	*workforce*
manœuvre (*m*)	*unskilled labourer*
négociant/ière (*m/f*)	*merchant*
ouvrier/ière (*m/f*) posté/e	*shiftworker*
patron/onne (*m/f*)	*boss*
patronat (*m*)	*the employers*
personnel (*m*)	*staff*
propriétaire (*m/f*)	*owner*
représentant/e (*m/f*)	*representative*
secrétaire (*f*) intérimaire	*temp*

un contrat de durée déterminée	*a short-term contract*
licencier des employés	*to lay off staff*
le président-directeur général (PDG)	*the managing director*
prendre# la retraite	*to retire*
faire# des études commerciales	*to do business studies*

LA VIE AU PAIR

accepter	*to accept*
s'adapter	*to settle down*
âge (*m*) minimum	*minimum age*
agence (*f*) au pair	*au pair agency*
aide (*f*) maternelle	*mother's help*

avoir# charge de	*to be in charge of*
avoir# droit à	*to be entitled to*
certificat (*m*) médical	*medical certificate*
conditions (*fpl*)	*requirements*
conditions (*fpl*) de travail	*working conditions*

55

connaissance (*f*) de langues	*language skills*
conseils (*mpl*)	*advice*
convenable	*suitable*
défrayer# quelqu'un	*to meet someone's expenses*
durée (*f*)	*duration*
essentiel/le	*essential*
expérimenté/e	*experienced*
faire# du babysitting	*to babysit*
fille (*f*) demi pair	*part-time au pair*
formulaire (*m*) de demande	*application form*
frais (*m*)	*expenses*
garder	*to watch over*
habituel/le	*routine*
jour (*m*) de congé	*day off*

lettre (*f*) de recommendation	*letter of recommendation*
logement (*m*) gratuit	*free lodgings*
obligeant/e	*helpful*
occasion (*f*)	*opportunity*
s'occuper de	*to look after*
pension (*f*) gratuite	*free board*
perfectionner	*to practise, to improve*
placement (*m*)	*position, post*
préavis (*m*)	*advance notice*
quotidien/ne	*daily*
responsable de	*responsible for*
séjour (*m*)	*stay*
sérieux/euse	*reliable*
les tâches (*fpl*) ménagères	*household tasks*

exiger# quelque chose de quelqu'un	*to require someone to do something*
suivre# des cours	*to attend classes*
perfectionner son français	*to practise/improve one's French*
se déclarer à la police	*to register with the police*
être# d'un grand secours	*to be very helpful*
nous exigeons deux références	*we require two references*
écrire# pour confirmer ces dispositions	*to write to confirm these arrangements*
un coupon-réponse international	*an international reply coupon*
s'arranger# avec quelqu'un pour faire quelque chose	*to arrange with someone to do something*
les modalités d'occupations	*the details of the work to be done*
être# en règle avec les autorités	*to have one's papers in order with the authorities*
prendre# les repas en commun	*to have meals with the family*
recevoir# une rétribution de	*to receive a payment of*

ADRESSES UTILES

Agence nationale pour l'emploi, Le Galillée, 4 rue Galillée, 93198 Noisy-le-Grand

Jeunes filles au pair, Relations internationales, 20 rue de l'exposition, 75007 Paris

Séjours internationaux linguistiques et culturels, 32 rempart de l'Est, 16022 Angoulème

Inter-Séjours, 179 rue Courcelles, 75017 Paris

LETTRES MODÈLES

1 Emploi au pair

Madame,

Je me mets en rapport avec vous au sujet d'un emploi au pair pour cet été.

J'aime beaucoup les enfants, et je serai heureuse de m'en occuper. Je voudrais également partager les tâches ménagères.

J'ai dix-huit ans et je termine mes études secondaires (j'étudie le français, l'histoire et les maths pour mon bac). Mon dernier examen aura lieu en juin, et je serai libre jusqu'en octobre, quand j'espère poursuivre mes études à l'université de Sheffield.

Si vous en avez besoin, je peux vous envoyer une lettre de recommandation.

Je vous prie, Madame, d'agréer l'expression de mes sentiments distingués.

2 Demande d'emploi

Monsieur,

Depuis le mois de juillet j'ai terminé mes études de français à l'université de Southampton, et je recherche activement un emploi en France pour perfectionner mon français.

J'apprends par le journal que vous envisagez embaucher... Je m'intéresse particulièrement au poste parce que..., je me permets, donc, de poser ma candidature à ce poste. Je suis libre dès maintenant. Je joins à cette lettre mon curriculum vitae et aussi l'adresse de deux personnes qui pourraient éventuellement vous fournir tous renseignements.

Dans l'espoir que ma demande retiendra votre attention, je vous prie d'agréer, Monsieur, l'expression de mes sentiments distingués.

3 Pour avoir des renseignements

Messieurs,

En ce moment je suis étudiant/e de français en Angleterre, et pour bien me préparer pour mes examens j'ai besoin de quelques renseignements au sujet de... Si vous avez des brochures ou d'autre documentation qui pourraient m'être utiles, je vous serais très reconnaissant/e de me les envoyer à l'adresse ci-dessus.

Je vous remercie à l'avance de l'attention que vous apporterez à cette demande, et vous prie de recevoir, Messieurs, l'expression de mes sentiments distingués.

LES PROBLÈMES SOCIAUX

LE CHÔMAGE

allocation (*f*) de chômage
unemployment benefit

augmentation (*f*) *increase*

blocage (*m*) des salaires *pay freeze*

bureau (*m*) d'embauche
unemployment office

chiffre (*m*) *figure*

chômage (*m*) des jeunes
youth unemployment

chômeur/euse (*m/f*)
unemployed person

confiance (*f*) en soi *self-confidence*

débaucher *to lay off staff*

dégradation (*f*) *worsening*

demandeur/euse (*m/f*) d'emploi
job-seeker

désœuvrement (*m*)
lack of anything to do

embauche (*f*) *vacancy*

ennui (*m*) *boredom*

facteur (*m*) *factor*

grève (*f*) *strike*

grève (*f*) du zèle *work-to-rule*

grève (*f*) patronale *lockout*

grève (*f*) totale *all-out strike*

gréviste (*m/f*) *striker*

impuissance (*f*) *powerlessness*

inactifs (*mpl*)
the numbers unemployed

jaune (*m*) *scab*

licenciement (*m*) *dismissal*

marché (*m*) de l'emploi
the jobs market

marché (*m*) du travail *labour market*

partage (*m*) de poste *job-sharing*

population (*f*) active
active population

préavis (*m*) de grève *strike notice*

respect (*m*) de soi *self-esteem*

robotisation (*f*) *automation*

sans-emploi (*mpl*) *the jobless*

statistiques (*fpl*) *statistics*

suppressions (*fpl*) d'emploi *jobs lost*

supprimer *to do away with*

taux (*m*) de chômage
unemployment level

travail (*m*) à temps partiel
part-time work

variation (*f*) saisonnière
seasonal variation

mettre# quelqu'un en chômage *to make someone redundant*

plan (*m*) de création d'emplois *job creation scheme*

décommander une grève *to call off a strike*

avoir# de l'impact sur	*to have an impact on*
les chômeurs de longue durée	*the long-term unemployed*
une diminution de la semaine de travail	*a reduction in the working week*
réduire# l'âge de la retraite	*to bring down the retirement age*
des entreprises en pleine mutation	*companies undergoing radical change*
s'inscrire# au chômage	*to sign on the dole*

LES SANS-ABRI

affamé/e	*starving*
Armée (f) du Salut	*Salvation Army*
aumône (f)	*handout*
bénévolat (m)	*voluntary help*
caritatif/ve	*charitable*
charité (f)	*charity*
cité (m) de transit	*(temporary) hostel*
clochard (m)	*tramp*
collecte (f) de fonds	*fund-raising*
déchéance (f)	*decline*
défavorisés (mpl)	*the disadvantaged*
dénuement (m)	*destitution*
désespoir (m)	*despair*
déshérités (mpl)	*the have-nots*
dignité (f)	*dignity*
exclusion (f) sociale	*social exclusion*
foyer (m)	*hostel*
gêne (f)	*financial difficulties*
gens (mpl) du voyage	*travellers (e.g. New Age)*
honte (f)	*shame*
indésirable	*undesirable*
malades (mpl) mentaux	*the mentally ill*

marginaliser	*to exclude from society*
marginaux (mpl)	*people living on the fringes of society*
mendicité (f)	*begging*
misère (f)	*extreme poverty, destitution*
musicien/ne (m/f) des rues	*busker*
nécessiteux/euse	*needy*
parasite (m)	*scrounger*
pauvreté (f)	*poverty*
personne (f) absente	*missing person*
quart monde (m)	*underclass*
quartiers (mpl) déshérités	*inner-city areas*
réinsertion (f)	*reintegration*
sans-abri (mpl)	*the homeless*
scandale (m)	*scandal*
seuil (m) de pauvreté	*poverty line*
société (f) d'abondance	*the affluent society*
soupe (f) populaire	*soup kitchen*
squatter	*to squat*
travail (m) social	*social work*
vulnérable	*vulnerable*

les naufragés de la conjoncture	*the casualties of the economic situation*
emménager# sur le bitume	*to live/sleep rough*
la ville se clochardise	*the town has more and more homeless people*
dormir# sous les ponts	*to live in cardboard boxes*
recevoir# l'aide sociale	*to be on social security*
hébergement (*m*) d'urgence	*emergency accommodation*
impropre à l'habitation	*not fit for human habitation*
Les SDF (sans domicile fixe)	*those of no fixed abode*
l'isolement (*m*) social	*social isolation*
faire# une fugue	*to run away from home*

LE CRIME

acte (*m*) délictueux	*criminal act*
affrontement (*m*)	*confrontation*
agresser	*to attack*
agresseur (*m*)	*attacker*
s'attaquer à	*to attack*
atteinte (*f*)	*attack*
bagarre (*f*)	*brawl*
balle (*f*)	*bullet*
braquage (*m*)	*hold-up*
braqueur (*m*)	*gangster*
brigade (*f*) criminelle	*crime squad*
butin (*m*)	*booty, haul*
cambriolage (*m*)	*burglary*
chantage (*m*)	*blackmail*
chasse (*f*) à l'homme	*manhunt*
châtiment (*m*)	*punishment*
chien (*m*) de défense	*guard dog*
commettre#	*to commit*

complice (*m/f*)	*accomplice*
crime (*m*) passionnel	*crime of passion*
CRS (*f*)	*riot police*
se défendre	*to defend oneself*
dégrader	*to damage*
délinquance (*f*)	*criminality*
délit (*m*)	*offence*
détenir#	*to hold prisoner*
dévaliser	*to burgle*
élucider	*to clear up, to solve*
émeute (*f*)	*riot*
en flagrant délit	*red-handed*
endommager#	*to damage*
enlèvement (*m*)	*kidnapping*
escroc (*m*)	*crook*
faire# irruption	*to burst in*
forces (*fpl*) de l'ordre	*police*
fraude (*f*) fiscale	*tax evasion*
fusillade (*f*)	*gunfire*

garde (f) à vue	*police custody*	recel (*m*)	*receiving stolen goods*
gardiennage (*m*)	*security*	règlement (*m*) de comptes	
groupe (*m*) d'autodéfense			*settling of scores*
	vigilante group	relâcher	*to set free*
incendie (*m*) criminel	*arson*	repris (*m*) de justice	*ex-convict*
injurier	*to insult*	saccager#	*to ransack*
intrus (*m*)	*intruder*	sévir	*to be rife*
ligoter	*to tie up*	tagueur (*m*)	*grafitti artist*
malfaiteur (*m*)	*criminal*	témoin (*m*)	*witness*
mobile (*m*)	*motive*	truand (*m*)	*crook*
otage (*m*)	*hostage*	vandalisme (*m*)	*vandalism*
pègre (f)	*underworld*	viol (*m*)	*rape*
poignarder	*to stab*	violation (f) de domicile	
prendre# la fuite	*to run away*		*forcible entry*
proxénétisme (*m*)	*pimping*	violer	*to rape*
punition (f) corporelle		vol (*m*) à l'étalage	*shoplifting*
	corporal punishment	vol (*m*) à la roulotte	*theft from cars*
racket (*m*)	*racketeering*	vol (*m*) à la tire	*pickpocketing*
rafle (f)	*police raid*	vol (*m*) à main armée	*armed robbery*
ravisseur/euse (*m/f*)		vols (*mpl*) de voiture	*car theft*
	kidnapper, abductor	voyou (*m*)	*hooligan*

faire# une virée	*to go joyriding*
prendre# en otage	*to take hostage*
la vague de criminalité	*the crime wave*
être# à l'abri de la violence	*to be safe from violence*
exercer# un effet de dissuasion	*to act as a deterrent*
entrer par effraction	*to break in*
dérober quelque chose à quelqu'un	*to steal something from someone*
se porter au secours de quelqu'un	*to go to someone's aid*
face à la recrudescence de la violence	*faced with the increased tide of violence*
déborder en violence	*to spill over into violence*

est-il souhaitable que la police soit armée? — *is it desirable to arm the police?*

agir sous l'emprise de l'alcool — *to act under the influence of alcohol*

la lutte contre le crime — *crime prevention*

LE TERRORISME

assassin (*m*)	*killer*
assassiner	*to murder*
atrocité (*f*)	*outrage*
attentat (*m*)	*attack*
attentat (*m*) à la bombe	*bomb attack*
balle (*f*)	*bullet*
bombe (*f*) télécommandée	*remote-controlled bomb*
cellule (*f*)	*(terrorist) cell*
cible (*f*)	*target*
dépister	*to track down*
désamorcer#	*to defuse*
détourner	*to hijack*
faire# sauter	*to blow up*
impitoyable	*ruthless*
indicateur (*m*) de police	*informer, supergrass*

innocent/e	*innocent*
mesures (*fpl*) de sécurité	*security measures*
militant/e (*m/f*)	*activist*
perpétrer#	*to carry out*
piégé/e	*booby-trapped*
plastiquer	*to carry out a bomb attack on*
plastiqueur (*m*)	*bomber*
reculer	*to back down*
sympathisant/e (*m/f*)	*sympathiser*
terroriste (*m/f*)	*terrorist*
tirer sur	*to open fire on*
tireur (*m*) isolé	*sniper*
voiture (*f*) piégée	*car-bomb*

faire# la grève de la faim	*to go on hunger strike*
créer des martyrs	*to create martyrs*
un meurtre commis de sang-froid	*a cold-blooded murder*
un acte délibéré de terrorisme	*a calculated act of terrorism*
prendre# des mesures énergiques contre	*to crack down on*
interdire# l'accès à	*to cordon off*
un attentat commis au hasard	*a random attack*
désamorcer une bombe	*to defuse a bomb*

faire# voler en éclats	*to blow to smithereens*
revendiquer la responsabilité de l'attentat	*to claim responsibility for the attack*
perpétrer# un attentat	*to carry out an attack*

LA JUSTICE

accusé/e (*m/f*)	*accused*
amende (*f*)	*fine*
arrêté (*m*) municipal	*bye-law*
atténuant/e	*mitigating*
attester	*to give evidence*
avocat/e (*m/f*)	*lawyer*
casier (*m*) judiciaire	*criminal record*
Code (*m*) Pénal	*penal code*
condamner	*to sentence*
contravention (*f*)	*motoring fine*
correctionnelle (*f*)	*magistrates' court*
cour (*f*) d'appel	*court of appeal*
cour (*f*) de cassation	*final court of appeal*
défenseur (*m*)	*defence counsel*
déposition (*f*)	*statement*
écrouer	*to imprison*
emprisonnement (*m*)	*imprisonment*
encourir# une peine	*to incur a fine*
être# sous les verrous	*to be behind bars*
incarcération (*f*)	*imprisonment*
inculper de	*to accuse of*
juge (*m*) d'instruction	*examining magistrate*

juridiquement	*legally*
libération (*f*) conditionnelle	*release on parole*
ordre (*m*) public	*law and order*
parquet (*m*)	*public prosecutor's office*
pénitentiaire	*prison (adj)*
plaider coupable	*to plead guilty*
plaidoirie (*f*)	*defence speech*
population (*f*) carcérale	*the prison population*
procès (*m*)	*trial*
processus (*m*) judiciaire	*legal process*
procureur (*m*)	*state prosecutor*
récidiver	*to reoffend*
récidiviste (*m*)	*habitual offender*
réclusion à perpétuité	*life imprisonment*
salle (*f*) d'audience	*courtroom*
sous caution	*on bail*
témoin (*m*)	*witness*
tribunal (*m*)	*court*
tribunal (*m*) correctionnel	*magistrates' court*
tribunal (*m*) pour enfants	*juvenile court*
venger#	*to avenge*

condamné/e à l'emprisonnement à perpétuité	*given a life sentence*
en détention provisoire	*remanded in custody*
comparaître# devant le tribunal	*to appear in court*
ouvrir# une information	*to start a preliminary investigation*
sanctionner une contravention	*to punish a crime*
un an de prison avec sursis	*a one-year suspended sentence*
le crime ne paie pas	*crime doesn't pay*
intenter un procès à	*to start proceedings against*

LA PEINE DE MORT

abolir	*to abolish*
appliquer	*to apply*
assassinat (*m*)	*murder*
barbare	*barbaric*
chaise (*f*) électrique	*electric chair*
châtiment (*m*) suprême	*supreme penalty*
chrétien/ne	*Christian*
condamnation (*f*) à mort	*death sentence*
à controverse	*controversial*
crime (*m*) odieux	*horrible crime*
crime (*m*) pendable	*hanging offence*
désaxé/e (*m/f*)	*unbalanced person*
dignité (*f*)	*dignity*

éliminer	*to eliminate*
exécution (*f*)	*execution*
faire# revivre	*to bring back to life*
guillotiner	*to send to the guillotine*
homicide (*m*) involontaire	*manslaughter*
irréversible	*irreversible*
maladie (*f*) mentale	*mental illness*
meurtrier/ière (*m/f*)	*murderer/murderess*
peine (*f*) capitale	*capital punishment*
pendaison (*f*)	*hanging*
punition (*f*)	*punishment*
rétablir	*to restore*
rétablissement (*m*)	*restoration, restoring*

avoir# un effet dissuasif sur	*to act as a deterrent for*
condamner quelqu'un à mort	*to condemn someone to death*
accorder une commutation de la peine capitale	*to grant a reprieve*
les infractions passibles de la peine de mort	*crimes which carry the death penalty*

avoir# une limite sur l'âge	*to have an age limit*
le droit de la société de se défendre	*society's right to defend itself*
une erreur judiciaire	*a miscarriage of justice*
le quartier des condamnés à mort	*'death row'*
des circonstances atténuantes	*mitigating circumstances*
supprimer la peine de mort	*to do away with the death penalty*

ADRESSES UTILES

Ministère de la Justice, 13 place Vendôme, 75042 Paris

Centre d'information civique, 242 bis boulevard Saint-Germain, 75006 Paris

Ministère du travail, de l'emploi et de la formation professionnelle, 127 rue de Grenelle, 75700 Paris

Secrétariat général pour l'administration de la police, 2 rue de la Cité, 75195 Paris

Secours populaire (SDF), 9-11 rue Froissart, 75003 Paris

Secours Catholique (SDF), 106 rue du Bac, 75341 Paris

Aide à toute détresse quart monde, 33 rue Bergère, 75009 Paris

CONSEIL DE VOCABULAIRE

Rappel – Pour bien apprendre du vocabulaire, il faut faire quelque chose d'actif.

Voici un petit jeu de vocabulaire. Choisissez 20 mots utiles dans une section (Prenons à titre d'exemple la section sur le chômage). Divisez les mots en deux (par exemple: chif fre, emb auche, grév iste). Mélangez les deux moitiés des mots et écrivez-les sur une feuille de papier, avec l'anglais à côté.

Exemple:

grév fre	*striker*
emb iste	*vacancy*
chif auche	*figure*

Mettez votre liste de 20 mots à côté pour un ou deux jours. Puis, essayez d'écrire la liste correctement en rejoignant les deux moitiés des mots.

Exemple:

grév fre	*striker = gréviste (m/f)*
emb iste	*vacancy = embauche (f)*
chif auche	*figure = chiffre (m)*

LA SANTÉ

LA DROGUE

abus (*m*) de la drogue — *drug abuse*

accoutumance (*f*) à la drogue — *drug habit*

accroché/e — *hooked*

acide (*m*) — *acid*

s'adonner à — *to become addicted to*

battage (*m*) — *hype*

brigade (*f*) des stupéfiants — *Drug Squad*

camé/e (*m/f*) — *junkie*

cannabis (*m*) — *cannabis*

cocaïne (*f*) — *cocaine*

colle (*f*) — *glue*

comateux /euse — *comatose*

consommateur/trice (*m*) de drogue — *drug-taker*

crack (*m*) — *crack*

dangerosité (*f*) — *level of danger*

dealer (*m*) — *drug pusher*

décrocher — *to come off drugs*

dépénaliser — *to decriminalise*

dépendance (*f*) de — *dependency on*

disponibilité (*f*) — *availability*

drogue (*f*) de synthèse — *designer drug*

drogue (*f*) douce/dure — *soft/hard drug*

drogue-partie (*f*) — *drugs party*

drogué/e (*m/f*) — *drug addict*

se droguer — *to take drugs*

enrayer# — *to curb, put a stop to*

euphorie (*f*) — *euphoria*

expérimentation (*f*) — *experimentation*

gélule (*f*) — *capsule*

hachisch (*m*) — *hashish*

hallucination (*f*) — *halllucination*

héroïne (*f*) — *heroin*

héroïnemanie (*f*) — *heroin addiction*

illicite — *illicit*

s'injecter — *to inject oneself*

légaliser — *to legalise*

marie-jeanne (*f*) — *pot*

marijuana (*m*) — *marijuana*

mondain/e — *fashionable*

overdose (*f*) — *overdose*

se piquer — *to inject oneself*

planer — *to be high on drugs*

poussée (*f*) de stupéfiants — *drug-pushing*

prise (*f*) — *seizure*

répandu/e — *widespread*

répression (*f*) contre — *crackdown on*

revendeur (*m*) de drogue — *drug peddler*

saisie (*f*) de drogue — *drugs haul*

sequelles (*fpl*) — *after-effects*

seringue (*f*) — *syringe*

se shooter à quelque chose — *to mainline something*

situation (*f*) de la drogue	*drug scene*	✳trafic (*m*) de la drogue	*drug-trafficking*
✳sniffeur (*m*)	*glue-sniffer*	trafiquant (*m*)	*drug smuggler*
✳stupéfiant (*m*)	*drug*	traitement (*m*)	*treatment*
✳toxico (toxicomane) (*m/f*)	*drug addict*	usage (*m*) de la drogue	*drug-taking*
✳toxicomanie (*f*)	*drug addiction*		

proposer de la drogue	*to offer drugs*
être# asservi à la drogue	*to be a slave to drugs*
une pente fatale	*a slippery slope*
se prémunir contre	*to guard against*
faire# un trip qui tourne mal	*to have a bad trip*
le désir de goûter au fruit défendu	*the wish to taste forbidden fruit*
s'échapper de la vie contemporaine	*to escape from modern life*
sombrer dans le désespoir	*to sink into despair*
lever# l'interdiction sur	*to lift the ban on*
la poursuite de nouvelles sensations	*the pursuit of new sensations*
reconnaître# les symptômes	*to spot the symptoms*
sniffer la colle	*to glue sniff*
subir un violent contre-coup physique	*to suffer violent physical after-effects*
l'usage de solvants hallucinogènes	*solvent abuse*
accusé de laxisme à l'égard des drogues	*accused of being too soft on drugs*
s'enfermer dans un cercle vicieux	*to get into a vicious circle*
être# en état de manque	*to experience withdrawal symptoms*

L'ALCOOL

✳alcoolique (*m/f*)	*alcoholic*	beuverie (*f*)	*drinking bout, binge*
✳alcoolisme (*m*)	*alcoholism*	✳boire# à l'excès	*to drink excessively*
Alcootest (*m*)	*Breathalyser*	boire# beaucoup	*to be a heavy drinker*
✳arroser	*to celebrate with alcohol*	✳boisson (*f*) alcoolisée	*alcoholic drink*
avertissement (*m*)	*warning*	boisson (*f*) légèrement alcoolisée	*low alcohol drink*

boisson (f) non alcoolisée	soft drink	inadaptation (f)	maladjustment
buveur/euse (m/f)	drinker	inhibition (f)	inhibition
canette (f) de bière	bottle of beer	ivresse (f)	drunkenness
cirrhose (f) du foie		ivrogne (m/f)	drunkard
	cirrhosis of the liver	sobre	sober
coordination (f)	co-ordination	taux (m) légal	legal limit
corser	to spike a drink	teneur (f) en alcool	alcoholic strength
dégriser	to sober up	tournée (f)	round of drinks
délier la langue	to loosen your tongue	trembler	to have the shakes
ébriété (f)	intoxication	trinquer à quelqu'un	to toast someone
s'enivrer	to get drunk	unité (f) d'alcool	unit of alcohol
éthylisme (m)	alcoholism	verre (m)	drink
s'évanouir	to blackout		
excessif/ve	excessive		

régime — *a diet*
régime sec — *alcohol free diet*

avec modération	in moderation
s'abstenir# de boire	to refrain from drink
l'alcool au volant	drink driving
le taux d'alcoolémie	alcohol level in the bloodstream
la consommation d'alcool par les mineurs	under-age drinking
faire# la tournée des pubs	to go on a pub crawl
perdre# tout contrôle de soi	to lose all self-control
être# en état d'ébriété	to be under the influence of alcohol
une personne qui ne boit jamais d'alcool	teetotaler
faire# régresser l'alcoolisme	to reduce alcoholism
enrayer# l'alcoolisme	to eliminate alcoholism
avoir# la gueule de bois	to have a hangover
les lois réglementant la vente d'alcool	the licensing laws
une cure de désintoxication	a drying-out treatment
en état d'ivresse publique	drunk and disorderly
facilement disponible	readily available

se faire - *to get help*

LE TABAC

altérer la santé   *to impair your health*

bronchite (*f*) chronique

chronic bronchitis

calmer les nerfs   *to calm one's nerves*

cancer (*m*) du poumon   *lung cancer*

dépendant/e de   *dependent upon*

difficulté (*f*) respiratoire

breathing difficulties

enfumer   *to fill with smoke*

espérance (*f*) de vie   *life expectancy*

éteindre#   *to extinguish*

fumeur/euse (*m/f*) invétéré/e

chain-smoker

gêner   *to disturb, bother*

habitude (*f*)   *habit*

haleine (*f*)   *breath*

haleter   *to gasp for breath*

la fumée ambiante - passive smoking
hors d'haleine - out of breath

inhaler   *to inhale*

interdiction (*f*)   *ban*

intoxiquer   *to poison*

lieu (*m*) collectif   *public place*

méfaits (*mpl*)   *ill effects*

néfaste   *harmful*

non-fumeur (*m*)   *non-smoker*

se passer de   *to do without*

patch (*m*)   *anti-smoking patch*

provoquer   *to cause*

rechuter   *to relapse*

régulièrement   *regularly*

supprimer   *to ban*

tabagisme (*m*)

addiction to smoking, nicotine addiction

taux (*m*) de nicotine   *nicotine level*

toux (*f*) de fumeur   *smoker's cough*

tousser - to cough

renoncer à - to give up

affirmer leur émancipation   *to prove their liberation*

la campagne anti-tabac   *the anti-smoking campaign*

essayer# de s'arrêter   *to try to give up*

le risque de mort subite   *the risk of sudden death*

chez les gros fumeurs   *for heavy smokers*

une méthode de sevrage tabagique   *a way of weaning people off smoking*

prévenir# les jeunes des dangers   *to warn young people of the dangers*

le respect pour son propre organisme   *respect for one's own body*

dissuader les jeunes de fumer   *to put young people off smoking*

le tabac est nuisible à la santé   *smoking is harmful to your health*

les affres du manque   *withdrawal symptoms*

agir sans aucun égard envers autrui   *to act without any consideration for other people*

LE SIDA

confiture – Jam

aiguille (*f*) souillée	*dirty needle*
contracter	*to catch*
dépistage (*m*)	*screening*
donneur/euse (*m/f*) de sang	
	blood donor
épargner	*to spare*
éthique	*ethical*
évitable	*avoidable*
éviter	*to avoid*
globule (*m*) blanc	*white blood cell*
guérissable	*curable*
hémophile (*m/f*)	*haemophiliac*
homosexuel	*homosexual*
hospice (*m*)	*hospice*
infecté/e	*infected*
infectieux/euse	*infectious*
irresponsable	*irresponsible*
partager#	*to share*
partenaires (*m/f*) multiples	
	multiple partners
population (*f*) à haut risque	
	high-risk group
porteur/euse (*m/f*)	*carrier*
pratiques (*mpl*) à risques	
	risky practices

Anti Corps – Antibodies:
Une épidémie – Empidemic

préservatif (*m*)	*condom*
préventif/ve	*preventive*
promiscuité (*f*)	*promiscuity*
se protéger#	*to protect oneself*
rapports (*mpl*) sexuels protégés	
	safe sex
relations (*fpl*) sexuelles	*intercourse*
séronégatif/ve	*HIV negative*
séropositif/ve	*HIV positive*
sexe (*m*) sans protection	
	unprotected sex
sidatique (*m/f*)	*AIDS victim*
sidéen/nne (*m/f*)	*AIDS sufferer*
survie (*f*)	*survival*
système (*m*) immunitaire	
	immune system
taux (*m*) de mortalité	*mortality rate*
transfusion (*f*) sanguine	
	blood transfusion
transmettre#	*to pass on*
transmission (*f*)	*transmission*
vaccin (*m*)	*vaccine*
victime (*f*)	*victim*
virus (*m*) HIV	*HIV virus*

Un remede   *remidies*

les personnes atteintes par le SIDA	*people suffering from AIDS*
la propagation du SIDA	*the spread of AIDS*
lancer# un programme de sensibilisation	*to launch an awareness programme*
s'activer à la recherche d'un vaccin	*to be busy trying to find a vaccine*
changer# souvent de partenaire	*to change partners frequently*

modifier les habitudes sexuelles	*to change sexual habits*
déconseiller à quelqu'un de faire quelque chose	*to advise against*

DIVERS

alité/e	*bedridden*
alléger#	*to relieve*
assurance (*f*) maladie	*health insurance*
atteint/e de	*suffering from*
automédication (*f*)	*self-medication*
aveugle	*blind*
avortée (*f*)	*woman who has had an abortion*
✱bébé-éprouvette (*m*)	*test-tube baby*
chercheur/euse (*m/f*)	*researcher*
chien-guide (*m*)	*guide dog*
chimiothérapie (*f*)	*chemotherapy*
chirurgie (*f*) esthétique	*cosmetic surgery*
chirurgie (*f*) réparatrice	*plastic surgery*
coma (*m*)	*coma*
cryogénie (*f*)	*cryogenics*
✱débrancher	*to switch off*
décéder#	*to die*
diagnostic (*m*)	*diagnosis*
✱douleur (*f*)	*pain*
embryon (*m*)	*embryo*
enceinte	*pregnant*
épave (*f*)	*human vegetable*
✱s'évanouir	*to faint*

Euthanésie   euthanasia

72

se faire# avorter	*to have an abortion*
fécondité (*f*)	*fertility*
fœtus (*m*)	*foetus*
frais (*mpl*) médicaux	*medical expenses*
génétique (*f*)	*genetics*
greffer	*to transplant*
guérir	*to cure*
guérisson (*f*)	*cure*
handicapé/e (*m/f*)	*handicapped person*
incapacité (*f*)	*disability*
inéluctable	*inevitable*
insupportable	*unbearable*
intervention (*f*)chirurgicale	*operation*
invalidité (*f*)	*disability*
irréversible	*irreversible*
issue (*f*) fatale	*fatal outcome*
lente agonie (*f*)	*lingering death*
litige (*m*)	*lawsuit*
malentendants (*mpl*)	*the hard of hearing*
malignant/e	*malignant*
mère (*f*) porteuse	*surrogate mother*
non-voyants (*mpl*)	*the non-sighted*
œuf (*m*) fécondé	*fertilised egg*
pénible	*painful*
perfusion (*f*)	*intravenous drip*
✱pilule (*f*)	*pill*

pis-aller (*m*)	*last resort*
prise (*f*) de sang	*blood sample/test*
prothèse (*f*)	*artificial limb*
rein (*m*) artificiel	*artificial kidney*
respirateur (*m*) artificiel	
	life-support machine
Sécu (*f*)	*Health Service*
souffrance (*f*)	*suffering*

sourd/e	*deaf*
stérilet (*m*)	*coil*
stimulateur (*m*) cardiaque	*pacemaker*
sujet (*m*) délicat	*emotive issue*
surmonter	*to overcome*
trisomique (*m/f*)	
	Down's syndrome sufferer

un centre de dépistage anticancéreux	*cancer screening unit*
le service de traumatologie	*casualty department*
disposer de son corps comme on veut	*to do what one likes with one's body*
supprimer un être humain	*to kill a human being*
une interruption volontaire de grossesse	*abortion*
une interruption thérapeutique de grossesse	*abortion on medical grounds*
la campagne contre l'avortement	*the anti-abortion campaign*
un avortement clandestin	*backstreet abortion*
réclamer le droit à l'euthanasie	*to demand the right to euthanasia*
une vie qui est à son terme	*a life which is at an end*
perdre# l'envie de vivre	*to lose the will to live*
être# atteint/e d'un mal incurable	*to suffer from an incurable illness*
être# en réanimation	*to be in intensive care*
revenir# à la conscience	*to regain consciousness*
l'acharnement thérapeutique	*unnatural prolongation of life*
mourir# dans la dignité	*to die with dignity*
les manipulations génétiques	*genetic engineering*
poser des problèmes éthiques	*to cause ethical problems*
le remède est pire que le mal	*the cure is worse than the disease*
la procréation artificielle	*artificial insemination*
une transplantation cardiaque	*a heart transplant*
ce médicament est remboursé par la Sécurité sociale	*the Health Service will reimburse you for the cost of this medicine*
la fécondation in vitro	*in vitro fertilisation*

ADRESSES UTILES

Haut Comité de la santé publique, 2 rue Auguste Comte, 92170 Vanves

Association nationale de prévention de l'alcoolisme, 20 rue Saint Fiacre, 75002 Paris

Ligue contre la fumée du tabac en public, 14 rue du Petit Ballon, 68000 Colmar

Fondation toxicomanie et prevention jeunesse, 38 rue du Texel, 75014 Paris

Centre d'étude et d'Information sur la toxicomanie, Centre Pey-Berland, 20 Place Pey-Berland, 33000 Bordeaux

(Abortion) Mouvement Initiative et Liberté, 4 rue Frédéric Mistral, 75015 Paris

Comité national contre le tabagisme, 66 rue de Binelles, 92310 Sèvres

Association nationale des centres d'interruption de grossesse et de contraception, 165 boulevard Aristide-Briand, 85000 La Roche-sur-Yon

Comité français d'éducation pour la santé, 22 rue Lecourbe, 75015 Paris

Association Jeunes Contre le Sida, 6 rue Dante, 75005 Paris

CONSEIL DE VOCABULAIRE

Trouvez-vous l'orthographe difficile? Essayez la méthode suivante:

a) Écrivez une liste de mots en anglais et en français, mais en remplaçant les lettres les plus difficiles des mots français avec des tirets. Par exemple:

artificial kidney   r_ _ n artifi_ _ _l

fertilised egg   o_ _ _ (f) f_con_ _

Regardez votre liste quelques jours plus tard. Pouvez-vous remplir les blancs?

b) Écrivez une liste de mots en français. Dans chaque mot vous faites une erreur d'orthographe exprès. Par exemple:

sangiun   *blood (adj)*

guérrissable   *curable*

Regardez votre liste quelques jours plus tard. Pouvez-vous trouver et corriger les erreurs? C'est un bon exercice qui vous apprend à trouver vos erreurs dans les dissertations avant votre professeur ou l'examinateur!

LE TEMPS LIBRE

LES SPORTS

adepte (*m/f*)	*enthusiast*
s'adonner à	*to go in for*
adresse (*f*)	*skill*
aduler	*to hero-worship*
adversaire (*m/f*)	*opponent*
amateurisme (*m*)	*amateurism*
argent (*m*) du prix	*prize money*
attrait (*m*)	*appeal*
battre# le record	*to beat the record*
bien-être (*m*)	*well-being*
bienfaisant/e	*beneficial*
bienfait (*m*)	*benefit*
championnat (*m*)	*championship*
classement (*m*)	*rankings, standings*
compatriote (*m/f*)	
	fellow countryman/woman
concurrent/e (*m/f*)	*competitor*
se consacrer à	*to devote oneself to*
contrôle (*m*) anti-dopage	*drug check*
corrompu/e	*corrupt*
débutant/e (*m/f*)	*beginner*
défaite (*f*)	*loss*
se défouler	*to let off steam*
démotiver	*to demotivate*
détente (*f*)	*relaxation*
disqualifier	*to disqualify*
droitier/ière	*right-handed*

éliminatoire	*preliminary*
entraînement (*m*)	*training*
équipement (*m*)	*equipment*
esprit (*m*) d'équipe	*team spirit*
étape (*f*)	*lap, stage*
évacuer les tensions	
	to get rid of tension
événement (*m*) sportif	*sporting event*
exercice (*m*)	*exercise*
exploitation (*f*)	*exploitation*
fanatique (*m/f*)	*fan*
foule (*f*)	*crowd*
gagnant/e (*m/f*)	*winner*
gaucher/ère	*left-handed*
haute compétition (*f*)	
	top-level competition
huer	*to boo*
inconditionnel/le (*m/f*)	*enthusiast*
se livrer à	*to devote oneself to*
ludique	*play (adj)*
maîtrise (*f*) de soi	*self-control*
maîtriser	*to master*
manche (*f*)	*round*
monnayer# son talent	
	to make money from one's talent
palme (*f*)	*prize*
passer professionnel	
	to turn professional
popularité (*f*)	*popularity*

pratiquer	*to practise, to do*
rajeunir	*to make you feel younger*
randonnée (*f*)	*hike, walking*
rapprocher	*to bring together*
règles (*fpl*)	*rules*
remporter le titre	*to win the title*
rencontre (*f*)	*fixture*
sain/e	*healthy*
spectateur/trice (*m/f*)	*spectator*
sport (*m*) d'équipe	*team sport*
sport (*m*) d'intérieur	*indoor sport*
sport (*m*) de masse	*very popular sport*
sport (*m*) de plein air	*outdoor sport*
sport (*m*) individuel	*individual sport*
sport-loisir (*m*)	*sport for all*
sportif/ve	*athletic*

sportivité (*f*)	*sportsmanship*
stage (*m*) de perfectionnement	
	advanced training course
succès (*m*)	*success*
se surpasser	*to excel oneself*
tactique (*f*)	*tactics*
toucher une prime	*to win a bonus*
tournoi (*m*)	*tournament*
transfert (*m*)	*transfer*
valorisation (*f*) de soi	
	increase in self-esteem
vedette (*f*) sportive	*sports star*
victoire (*f*)	*win*
vie (*f*) sédentaire	
	life at a desk, inactive life
vieillissement (*m*)	*growing old*

se livrer à une activité	*to involve oneself in an activity*
les stéroïdes anabolisants	*anabolic steroids*
détenir# le record mondial	*to hold the world record*
mélanger# le sport et la politique	*to mix sport and politics*
pour parvenir# au sommet	*to reach the top*
une carrière de courte durée	*a short-lived career*
se libérer# de son énergie en excès	*to work off one's excess energy*
compromettre# sa santé	*to put one's health at risk*

LES PASSE-TEMPS

agréable	*enjoyable*
amitié (*f*)	*friendship*
boîte (*f*) de nuit	*night club*
bricolage (*m*)	*DIY*

casanier/ière	*stay-at-home*
centre (*m*) de loisirs	*leisure centre*
collectionner	*to collect*
cours (*m*) du soir	*evening class*
délassement (*m*)	*relaxation*

distraction (*f*)	*amusement*
divertissement (*m*)	*relaxation, entertainment*
doué/e	*gifted*
engouement (*m*) pour	*craze for*
exceller à	*to excel at*
facultatif/ve	*optional*
foyer (*m*) des jeunes	*youth club*
industrie (*f*) des loisirs	*entertainment industry*

installations (*fpl*)	*facilities*
intérêt (*m*)	*interest*
jardinage (*m*)	*gardening*
oisiveté (*f*)	*idleness*
se passionner pour	*to be really keen on*
profiter de	*to take advantage of*
progrès (*mpl*) personnels	*self-improvement*
temps (*m*) libre	*free time*

la valorisation de soi	*increase in self-esteem*
à la portée de tout le monde	*accessible for everyone*
s'occuper l'esprit	*to keep one's mind active*
être# bien dans sa peau	*to feel happy and fulfilled*
la diminution du temps de travail	*the reduction in working hours*
les agréments de la vie	*the pleasures of life*
trouver du plaisir à faire quelque chose	*to derive enjoyment from doing something*
un passe-temps qui en vaut la peine	*a rewarding hobby*

LE TOURISME

à ne pas manquer	*not to be missed*
accueil (*m*)	*welcome*
actif/ve	*active*
afflux (*m*)	*flood (of people)*
animé/e	*lively*
aoûtien/ne (*m/f*)	*August holiday-maker*
attrape-touristes (*m*)	*tourist trap*
aventureux/euse	*adventurous*
se baser à	*to be based in*

la belle saison	*summer months*
bronzage (*m*)	*suntan*
bronzage (*m*) intégral	*all-over tan*
circuit (*m*) touristique	*tourist circuit*
complexe (*m*) touristique	*tourist complex*
compliqué/e	*complicated*
croisière (*f*)	*cruise*
découverte (*f*)	*discovery*
déçu/e	*disappointed*
départ (*m*)	*departure*

déplacement (*m*)	*trip*	paradis (*m*)	*paradise*
éloigné/e	*far off*	pittoresque	*picturesque*
estival/e	*summer (adj)*	propriété (*f*) à temps partagé	
estivant/e (*m/f*)	*summer visitor*		*time-share flat*
étaler	*to stagger (holidays)*	proximité (*f*)	*nearness*
évasion (*f*)	*escape*	récupérer	*to recover*
explorer	*to explore*	rentrée (*f*)	*return from holidays*
faire# du tourisme	*to go sightseeing*	résidence (*f*) secondaire	*holiday home*
faire# étape	*to break the journey*	retour (*m*) à la nature	*back to nature*
farniente (*m*)	*lazing around*	réussi/e	*successful*
fin (*f*) de saison	*end of season*	séjour (*m*) balnéaire	*seaside stay*
folie (*f*)	*madness*	site (*m*)	*beauty spot*
gîte (*m*)	*self-catering home*	station (*f*) de sports d'hiver	
guide (*m*) agréé	*qualified guide*		*winter sports resort*
hébergement (*m*)	*accommodation*	station (*f*) familiale	*family resort*
hivernant/e (*m/f*)	*winter visitor*	vacances (*fpl*) à thème	
industrie (*f*) du tourisme			*special interest holidays*
	tourist industry	vacancier/ière (*m/f*)	*holiday-maker*
inoubliable	*unforgettable*	valeur (*f*) éducative	*educational value*
juilletiste (*m/f*)	*July holiday-maker*	vie (*f*) nocturne	*night life*
lieu (*m*) à la mode	*a fashionable place*	villégiature (*f*)	*holiday*
location (*f*)	*rent, hire*	visite (*f*) d'échange	*exchange visit*
lointain/e	*distant*	voyage (*m*) d'agrément	*pleasure trip*
manière (*f*) de vivre	*way of life*	voyage (*m*) organisé	*package holiday*
morte-saison (*f*)	*off-season*	voyages (*mpl*)	*travelling*
nuitées (*fpl*)	*overnight stays*	weekend (*m*) prolongé	
			extended weekend

faire# le pont	*to make a long weekend of it*
les vacances de Pâques se déroulent tôt cette année	*the Easter holidays fall early this year*
le premier pays touristique du monde	*the world's number one tourist destination*

la formule de soleil, sable et sexe reste populaire	*sun, sand and sex remains a popular recipe*
élargir ses horizons	*to broaden one's outlook*
avoir# envie de voir le monde	*to have the travel bug*
aller# à la recherche du soleil	*to go in search of some sun*
pour accueillir# le déferlement de vacanciers	*to cope with the flood of holidaymakers*
les vacances, c'est la soupape de sécurité	*holidays are a safety valve*
estamper les touristes	*to fleece the tourists*
l'exode de Paris	*the mass departure from Paris*
dégagé/e des contraintes quotidiennes	*away from the daily grind*
rayonner dans une région	*to tour around an area from a base*
favoriser l'entente entre les pays	*to further understanding between countries*
avoir# une valeur éducative	*to be of educational value*
recharger# les batteries	*to recharge one's batteries*

ADRESSES UTILES

Ministère du tourisme, 101 rue de Grenelle, 75007 Paris

Agence nationale de l'information touristique, 8 avenue de l'Opéra, 75041 Paris

Ministère de la jeunesse et des sports, 78 rue Olivier-de-Serres, 75015 Paris

Accueil des jeunes en France, 12 rue des Barres, 75004 Paris

CONSEIL DE VOCABULAIRE

Rappel – Pour bien apprendre du vocabulaire, il faut faire quelque chose d'actif. C'est en forgeant qu'on devient forgeron!

Rédigez pour vous-même ou pour un/e ami/e un quiz sur le nouveau vocabulaire. L'acte même d'écrire le quiz, aussi bien que l'acte de le résoudre, aide à renforcer les mots. Voici quelques exemples de la sorte de question qu'on pourrait poser:

a) Quel «B»me donne 'sunbathing' en français?   (Réponse – *bronzage*)

b) Quel mot manque dans cette phrase? «A pleasure trip = Un voyage d'_____» (Réponse – *agrément*)

c) Quel est le contraire d'«un estivant»?   (Réponse – *un hivernant*)

d) Quel mot est l'intrus? «Délassement, temps libre, affaires»?
(Réponse – *affaires, parce que c'est du travail et pas de la détente*).

UN TOUR DU MONDE

LA GUERRE ET LA PAIX

abri (*m*)	*shelter*
alliés (*mpl*)	*allies*
ancien combattant (*m*)	*war veteran*
armée (*f*) de métier	*professional army*
aviation (*f*) coalisée	*allied aircraft*
aviation (*f*) de combat	*fighter force*
blocus (*m*)	*blockade*
capituler	*to surrender*
cessez-le-feu (*m*)	*ceasefire*
combats (*mpl*) acharnés	*heavy fighting*
conférence (*f*) de paix	*peace conference*
conflit (*m*)	*conflict*
conquérir	*to conquer*
contrôle (*m*) des armements	*arms control*
course (*f*) aux armements	*arms race*
défaite (*f*)	*defeat*
désarmement (*m*) unilatéral	*unilateral disarmament*
détestable	*appalling*
effectuer un raid	*to carry out a raid*
embargo (*m*)	*embargo*
s'emparer de	*to seize*
en guerre	*at war*
engager#	*to enlist*

entre-deux-guerres (*m*)	*inter-war years*
envahir	*to invade*
escalade (*f*)	*escalation*
état (*m*) des pertes	*casualty list*
éviter	*to avoid*
fabricant (*m*) d'armes	*arms manufacturer*
faire# la guerre à	*to wage war on*
force (*f*) de frappe	*strike force*
forces (*fpl*) armées	*armed forces*
fusée (*f*)	*rocket*
guerre (*f*) chimique	*chemical warfare*
guerre (*f*) civile	*civil war*
guerre (*f*) d'embuscade	*guerrilla warfare*
guerre (*f*) mondiale	*world war*
guerre (*f*) nucléaire	*nuclear war*
hélicoptère (*m*) de combat	*helicopter gunship*
initiative (*f*) de paix	*peace initiative*
lancer#	*to launch*
manifestation (*f*) pacifiste	*peace march*
manœuvres (*fpl*)	*manoeuvres*
mater	*to subdue, quell*
matériel (*m*) de guerre	*weaponry*
missile (*m*) à longue portée	*long-range missile*

mutilés (*mpl*) de guerre	*war-disabled*
neutre	*neutral*
objecteur (*m*) de conscience	
	conscientious objector
ogive (*f*) nucléaire	*nuclear warhead*
pacifique	*peaceful, peace-loving*
pacifiste (*m/f*)	*pacifist*
paix (*f*)	*peace*
porte-avions (*m*)	*aircraft carrier*
pourparlers (*mpl*) de paix	*peace talks*
prendre# d'assaut	*to take by storm*

préventif/ve	*pre-emptive*
prolifération (*f*) nucléaire	
	nuclear proliferation
purification (*f*) ethnique	
	ethnic cleansing
service (*m*) militaire	*military service*
solution (*f*) négociée	
	negotiated settlement
superpuissances (*fpl*)	*super-powers*
trêve (*f*)	*truce*

déchiré/e par la guerre	*war-torn*
recourir# à la force	*to resort to force*
être# dans une position de force	*to be in a position of strength*
la force de dissuasion nucléaire	*the nuclear deterrent*
les forces de maintien de la paix	*peace-keeping forces*
un pays détenteur d'armes nucléaires	*a country which possesses nuclear weapons*
la raison du plus fort est toujours la meilleure	*might is right*
vivre# dans la peur d'une nouvelle guerre	*to live in fear of another war*
il y a eu de nombreuses victimes	*there were heavy casualties*
la guerre dans toute sa laideur	*the full horror of war*
appliquer des sanctions économiques	*to apply economic sanctions*
faire# son service militaire	*to do one's military service*

LA RELIGION

adepte (*m/f*)	*follower*
adorer	*to worship*

s'agenouiller	*to kneel (down)*
agnostique (*m/f*)	*agnostic*
aller# à l'église	*to go to church*

âme (*f*)	*soul*
ange (*m*)	*angel*
assistance (*f*)	*congregation*
astrologie (*f*)	*astrology*
athée (*m/f*)	*atheist*
athéisme (*m*)	*atheism*
au-delà (*m*)	*afterworld*
bénir	*to bless*
Bible (*f*)	*Bible*
Bouddhisme (*m*)	*Buddhism*
Carême (*m*)	*Lent*
catholicisme (*m*)	*Catholicism*
chaire (*f*)	*pulpit*
chrétien/ne (*m/f*)	*Christian*
christianiser	*to convert to Christianity*
christianisme (*m*)	*Christianity*
ciel (*m*)	*heaven*
convertir à	*to convert to*
Coran (*m*)	*Koran*
croire# en Dieu	*to believe in God*
croix (*f*)	*cross*
croyances (*fpl*) religieuses	*religious beliefs*
croyant/e (*m/f*)	*believer*
culte (*m*)	*worship*
diable (*m*)	*devil*
Église (*f*) orthodoxe	*Orthodox Church*
enfer (*m*)	*hell*
espoir (*m*)	*hope*
évangéliste (*m/f*)	*born-again Christian*
évêque (*m*)	*bishop*

extrémisme (*m*) islamique	*islamic extremism*
fidèles (*mpl*)	*the faithful*
foi (*f*)	*faith*
immortalité (*f*)	*immortality*
intégriste (*m/f*)	*fundamentalist*
islam (*m*)	*Islam*
jour (*m*) du seigneur	*the Lord's Day*
juif/juive (*m/f*)	*Jew*
matérialisme (*m*)	*materialism*
messe (*f*)	*mass*
mœurs (*fpl*)	*morals*
mosquée (*f*)	*mosque*
musulman/e (*m/f*)	*Muslim*
office (*f*)	*service*
pape (*m*)	*Pope*
paroisse (*f*)	*parish*
pécheur/pécheresse (*m/f*)	*sinner*
péché (*m*)	*sin*
prêcher	*to preach*
prédication (*f*)	*preaching, sermon*
présent (*m*)	*the here and now*
prière (*f*)	*prayer*
profane	*secular*
rabbin (*m*)	*rabbi*
réconforter	*to comfort*
sacerdotal	*priestly*
Sainte Vierge (*f*)	*Virgin Mary*
salut (*m*)	*salvation*
secte (*f*)	*sect*
sens (*m*) de la vie	*meaning of life*
superstition (*f*)	*superstition*

synagogue (*f*)	*synagogue*	Témoin (*m*) de Jéhovah	
système (*m*) de valeurs			*Jehovah's witness*
	system of values	vaudou (*m*)	*voodoo*

l'infaillibilité pontificale	*papal infallibility*
croire# à la vie après la mort	*to believe in life after death*
être# enseveli/e chrétiennement	*to have a Christian burial*
prier Dieu de faire un miracle	*to pray for a miracle*
il n'est plus pratiquant	*he doesn't go to church any more*
un catholique qui n'est plus pratiquant	*a lapsed Catholic*
la poussée de l'Islam	*the upsurge of Islam*
se détourner de la religion	*to turn away from religion*
la prise de position morale de l'Église	*the Church's moral standpoint*
la méditation transcendantale	*transcendental meditation*
abandonner le culte	*to give up one's religion*
se tourner vers la religion	*to turn to religion*

LE TIERS-MONDE

affamé/e	*starving*	défavorisé/e	*underprivileged*
agoniser	*to be dying*	denrées (*fpl*)	*food supplies*
aide (*f*) alimentaire	*food aid*	dénué/e de tout	*destitute*
aide (*f*) au développement		déshérité/e	*deprived*
	development aid	disette (*f*)	*food shortage*
aide (*f*) étrangère	*foreign aid*	durable	*lasting*
aide (*f*) humanitaire	*humanitarian aid*	eau (*f*) potable	*drinking water*
aide (*f*) liée	*tied aid*	endetté/e	*in debt*
alléger#	*to lessen, to relieve*	espérance (*f*) de vie	*life expectancy*
s'appauvrir	*to grow poorer*	exploiter	*to exploit*
bidonville (*m*)	*shanty town*	impuissant/e	*powerless*
corruption (*f*)	*corruption*	inégalité (*f*)	*inequality*
crise (*f*)	*crisis*	installations (*fpl*) sanitaires	*sanitation*
		insuffisant/e	*inadequate*

83

irriguer	*to irrigate*
les moins nantis	*the less well-off*
maladie (*f*)	*disease*
malédiction (*f*)	*curse*
malnutrition (*f*) aiguë	*chronic malnutrition*
matières (*fpl*) premières *raw materials*	
mendier	*to beg (for)*
mousson (*f*)	*monsoon*
Occident (*m*)	*the West*
octroyer# de l'aide	*to grant aid*
opprimé/e	*oppressed*
pays (*m*) donateur	*donor country*
pays (*m*) industrialisé	*industrialised country*
pays (*mpl*) occidentaux	*western countries*
piller	*to pillage*

régime (*m*) corrompu	*corrupt regime*
régulation (*f*) des naissances	*birth control*
retard (*m*) économique	*economic backwardness*
société (*f*) de secours	*relief organisation*
sort (*m*)	*fate*
souffrance (*f*)	*suffering*
sous-alimenté/e	*under-nourished*
sous-développé/e	*under-developed*
surexploitation (*f*)	*over-exploitation*
surpopulation (*f*)	*over-population*
suspension (*f*) de l'aide	*suspension of aid*
taudis (*m*)	*slum*
taux (*m*) de mortalité	*mortality rate*

lancer# un appel aux pays riches	*to appeal to the rich countries*
s'atteler# à promouvoir le développement	*to get down to promoting development*
le soulagement de la misère	*the relief of poverty*
l'alphabétisation de la population	*teaching people to read and write*
financer# des programmes de développement	*to finance development programmes*
un pays en voie de développement	*developing country*
parrainer un enfant	*to sponsor a child*
l'espoir d'un avenir meilleur	*the hope of a better future*
privilégier# la santé	*to give greater importance to health*
laisser le pays exsangue	*to bleed the country dry*
un représentant d'un organisme humanitaire	*aid-worker*
alléger# la souffrance	*to relieve suffering*

se tirer de la misère par leurs propres
efforts — *to escape poverty by their own efforts*

le droit des peuples à se nourrir
eux-mêmes — *the right of nations to feed themselves*

LES CATASTROPHES

abattre#	*to knock down*
s'affaisser	*to collapse, to give way*
affligé/e	*distressed*
anéantir	*to annihilate*
angoisse (*f*)	*distress*
arracher	*to uproot*
atteint/e	*affected*
avertissement (*m*)	*warning*
boîte (*f*) noire	*black box*
brasier (*m*)	*inferno*
broyer#	*to crush*
cadavre (*m*)	*corpse*
calciné/e	*charred, burnt to a cinder*
carambolage (*m*)	*pile-up*
catastrophe (*f*) naturelle	*natural disaster*
cauchemar (*m*)	*nightmare*
chapelle (*f*) ardente	*chapel of rest*
condoléances (*fpl*)	*sympathy*
couler	*to sink*
coupure (*f*) de courant	*power cut*
déblayage (*m*)	*clearing up*
décombres (*mpl*)	*debris, rubble*
déflagration (*f*)	*explosion*
défoncer#	*to smash in*

dégager#	*to free*
dégâts (*mpl*)	*damage*
détruire#	*to destroy*
deuil (*m*)	*mourning*
dévasté/e	*devastated*
disette (*f*)	*food shortage*
écraser	*to squash*
s'écraser	*to crash*
s'effondrer	*to collapse*
ensevelir	*to bury*
épauler	*to back up, support*
épave (*f*)	*wreck*
erreur (*f*) humaine	*human error*
éruption (*f*)	*outbreak*
évacuer	*to evacuate*
exploser	*to explode*
funèbre	*gloomy, dismal*
gravats (*mpl*)	*rubble (small pieces)*
grièvement	*seriously*
heurter	*to strike*
hospitaliser	*to take to hospital*
incendie (*m*)	*fire*
indemne	*unhurt*
inondation (*f*)	*flood*
naufrage (*m*)	*shipwreck*
navrant/e	*heartbreaking*

percuter (contre)	*to crash into*
périr	*to perish*
ravager#	*to devastate*
règles (*fpl*) de sécurité	*safety rules*
repêcher	*to recover (bodies)*
rescapé/e (*m/f*)	*survivor*
sain/e et sauf/ve	*safe and sound*
sanglant/e	*bloody*
sauvetage (*m*)	*rescue*
sauveteur (*m*)	*rescuer*
sécheresse (*f*)	*drought*
secousse (*f*)	*shock*
séisme (*m*)	*earthquake*
sinistre (*m*)	*disaster*
sinistré/e	*disaster-stricken*
sinistré/e (*m/f*)	*disaster victim*
sombrer	*to sink*
tragédie (*f*)	*tragedy*
tremblement (*m*) de terre	*earthquake*
victime (*f*)	*victim*
vivant/e	*alive*
zone (*f*) sinistrée	*disaster area*

provoquer la mort de trois personnes	*to cause the death of three people*
d'après les derniers chiffres	*according to the latest figures*
évaluer le montant des dégâts	*to work out the total amount of damage*
le vent attise les feux	*the wind is fanning the flames*
dépêcher sur les lieux	*to dispatch to the scene*
travailler sans relâche	*to work non-stop*
lancer# un appel d'urgence	*to launch an emergency appeal*
déclarer l'état d'urgence	*to declare a state of emergency*
le bilan provisoire	*the provisional death-toll*
le bilan définitif	*the final death-toll*

LA UE

adhérer# à	*to belong to*
affecter des crédits	*to allocate funds*
barrière (*f*) douanière	*customs barrier*
bureaucratie (*f*)	*bureaucracy*
céder#	*to give way*
clause (*f*) d'exemption	*opt-out clause*
communauté (*f*)	*community*
député (*m*) européen	*Euro MP*
eurocrate (*m/f*)	*Eurocrat (EU employee)*
Europe des douze	*the Twelve*
eurosceptique (*m/f*)	*eurosceptic*
fédéral/e	*federal*
frontalier/ière	*border (adj)*
libre circulation (*f*)	*freedom of movement*

Marché (*m*) commun	*Common Market*
marché (*m*) unique	*single market*
monnaie (*f*) unique	*single currency*
négocier	*to negotiate*
parlement (*m*) européen	*European Parliament*
passer la frontière	*to cross the border*
pays (*m*) membre	*member country*
pays (*m*) voisin	*neighbouring country*
présidence (*f*)	*presidency*

ressortissant/e (*m/f*)	*citizen*
souveraineté (*f*)	*sovereignty*
subventionner	*to subsidise*
traité (*m*)	*treaty*
transfrontalier/ière	*cross-border*
union (*f*) européenne	*European Union*
union (*f*) monétaire	*monetary union*
vote (*m*) majoritaire	*majority voting*

la libre circulation des travailleurs	*free movement of labour*
la politique agricole commune	*Common Agricultural Policy*
respecter les directives de la UE	*to follow EU directives*
les règlements de la UE	*EU regulations*
l'harmonisation communautaire	*community-wide standardisation*
être# profondément divisé/e par	*to be deeply divided by*
rendre# la Communauté plus apte à	*to make the Community more capable of*
l'adhésion au Marché commun	*membership of the Common Market*
envisager# l'élargissement de la Communauté	*to envisage widening the Community*
renforcer# le sentiment européen	*to strengthen European feeling*
concerter l'action	*to act together*
craindre# la perte de l'identité nationale	*to fear the loss of national identity*
se montrer très européen/ne	*to be pro-European*
la monnaie est en danger	*the currency is under threat*

LE LOGEMENT

agent (*m*) immobilier	*estate agent*
aménager	*to convert*
ameublement (*m*)	*furnishing*
bâtir	*to build*

béton (*m*)	*concrete*
chantier (*m*)	*building-site*
construire#	*to construct, build*
crise (*f*) du logement	*housing shortage*

délabré/e	*dilapidated*
déménager#	*to move house*
domicile (*m*)	*home, residence*
emménager#	*to move in*
foncier/ière	*land (adj)*
habitat (*m*)	*housing conditions*
immeuble (*m*)	*block of flats*
immobilier (*m*)	*property business*
industrie (*f*) du bâtiment	
	building industry
locataire (*m/f*)	*tenant*
maison-modèle (*f*)	*show house*
malsain/e	*unhealthy*
mètre (*m*) carré	*square metre*
occupant (*m*) propriétaire	
	owner-occupier

pénurie (*f*)	*shortage*
propriété (*f*)	*property*
réhabiliter	*to restore*
relogement (*m*)	*rehousing*
rénovation (*f*)	*renovation*
résidence (*f*) principale	*main home*
résidence (*f*) secondaire	
	holiday home
retaper	*to do up*
spacieux/euse	*roomy*
squatter	*to squat*
statut (*m*) social	*social status*
taudis (*m*)	*slum*
terrain (*m*)	*building plot*
vétuste	*old and dilapidated*

les conditions de vie	*living conditions*
la contrainte économique	*economic constraint*
un cadre de vie	*a living environment*
les familles à revenu moyen	*families on average income*
l'urbanisation sauvage	*unplanned building*
le placement pierre	*investment in bricks and mortar*
charbonnier est maître dans sa maison	*you are master in your own home*
être# propriétaire	*to be a home-owner*
la France profonde	*the broad mass of French people*

EN VILLE

agglomération (*f*)	*built-up area*
aire (*f*) de jeux	*adventure playground*

animation (*f*)	*bustle*
anonymat (*m*)	*anonymity*
arrondissement (*m*)	*district*

banlieue (*f*)	*suburb*	quartier (*m*)	*neighbourhood*
banlieusard/e (*m/f*)	*commuter*	quartier (*m*) résidentiel	
bitume (*m*)	*asphalt*		*residential area*
brouhaha (*m*)	*hubbub*	repeupler	*to repopulate*
cadre (*m*)	*setting*	se ressembler	*to look alike*
ceinture (*f*) verte	*green belt*	rues (*fpl*) piétonnes	
citadin/e (*m/f*)	*city dweller*		*pedestrianised streets*
cité (*f*)	*estate*	sans âme (*f*)	*soulless*
cité (*f*) ouvrière	*housing estate*	services (*mpl*) publics	*public services*
ensemble (*m*)	*housing scheme*	sortie (*f*) de la ville	*edge of town*
s'entasser	*to cram together*	stressé/e	*stressful*
espace (*m*) vert	*green space, park*	surpeuplé/e	*overcrowded*
faire# la navette	*to commute*	terrain (*m*) vague	*waste ground*
faubourg (*m*)	*inner suburb*	trépidant/e	*hectic*
fond (*m*) sonore	*background noise*	tristesse (*f*)	*sadness*
gratte-ciel (*m*)	*skyscraper*	s'urbaniser	*to become built-up*
HLM (*f*)	*council flat*	urbanisme (*m*)	*town planning*
labyrinthe (*m*)	*maze, rabbit-warren*	urbaniste (*m*)	*town planner*
laideur (*f*)	*ugliness*	ville (*f*) satellite	*satellite town*
loyer (*m*)	*rent*	ville-dortoir (*f*)	*dormitory town*
mobilier (*m*) urbain	*street furniture*	voisinage (*m*)	*neighbourhood*
périphérique	*outlying*	zone (*f*) d'activités	*business park*
prospère	*prosperous*	zone (*f*) piétonnière	
			pedestrian precinct

la densité de la population	*population density*
faire# partie du charme de la ville	*to add to the charm of the town*
la situation dans les banlieues à problèmes est intenable	*the situation in the problem suburbs is intolerable*
une ville sans agrément	*an unattractive town*
situé/e dans un cadre de verdure	*in a leafy setting*

LA CAMPAGNE

abords (*mpl*)	*surroundings*
agrément (*m*)	*charm*
alentours (*mpl*)	*surroundings, vicinity*
ambiance (*f*)	*atmosphere*
calme (*m*)	*calm*
campagnard/e (*m/f*)	*country dweller*
communauté (*f*)	*community*
commune (*f*)	*district*
décroître#	*to decrease*
dépaysement (*m*)	*disorientation*
dépeuplement (*m*)	*depopulation*
éloignement (*m*)	*distance*
endormi/e	*sleepy*
équipements (*mpl*)	*facilities*
exode (*m*) rural	*drift from the land*
idylle (*f*)	*idyll*

s'implanter	*to settle*
infrastructure (*f*)	*infrastructure*
isolé/e	*cut off, isolated*
mieux-vivre (*m*)	*improved standard of living*
mode (*m*) de vie	*way of life*
mythe (*m*)	*myth*
nature (*f*)	*nature*
paisible	*peaceful*
pittoresque	*picturesque*
région (*f*) arriérée	*backward area*
reposant/e	*restful*
site (*m*) protégé	*preservation area*
survie (*f*) du village	*survival of the village*
verdure (*f*)	*greenery*
vie (*f*) villageoise	*village life*

faire# quelque chose à son rythme	*to do something at one's own pace*
jouir de la paix	*to enjoy the peace*
s'exiler à la campagne	*to bury oneself in the country*
les changements survenus dans l'agriculture	*changes that have come about in agriculture*
la campagne dépeuplée	*the deserted countryside*
habiter en plein bled	*to live in the middle of nowhere*

ADRESSES UTILES

Prévention des accidents domestiques, Boîte Postale 71, 93151 Le Blanc Mesnil

Euroguichet, Rue de la République 16, 69289 Lyon

Centre d'information et de documentation religieuses, 6 place du Parvis-Notre-Dame, 75004 Paris

ONU, 4-6 avenue de Saxe, 75700 Paris

Bureau d'information des communautés européennes, 61 rue des Belles-Feuilles, 75116 Paris

Amnesty International, 4 rue de la Pierre-Levée, 75011 Paris

Médecins du monde, 67 avenue de la République, 75011 Paris

Médecins sans frontières, 8 rue Saint-Sabin, 75011 Paris

Jeunesse pour l'Europe, 2-3 Place du Luxembourg, 1040 Bruxelles, Belgium

Centre de documentation Tiers Monde, 20 rue Rochechouart, 75009 Paris

Unesco, 1 rue Miollis, 75015 Paris

CONSEIL DE VOCABULAIRE

Rappel – Pour bien apprendre du vocabulaire, il faut faire quelque chose d'actif. C'est en forgeant qu'on devient forgeron!

Est-ce que vous pouvez bien juger les connaissances de vocabulaire d'un(e) partenaire? Faites un jeu de prédiction. Choisissez un thème que vous avez étudié (ici on prend l'exemple des catastrophes). Faites trois listes. Chaque liste a dix mots en anglais. La première contient les mots faciles. Vous êtes sûr que votre partenaire connaît le français. La deuxième contient les mots les plus utiles – ceux que votre partenaire devrait connaître. La troisième contient des mots difficiles – vous êtes presque certain que votre partenaire ne les connaît pas. Vous échangez de listes, et vous regardez si vous avez bien prédit les connaissances de vocabulaire de votre partenaire.

Par exemple:

Liste facile: to explode, alive, to evacuate, victim, etc.

Liste utile: corpse, warning, unhurt, debris, etc.

Liste difficile: heart-breaking, to annihilate, gloomy, rubble, etc.

CONCLUSION

LES PHRASES

1 Essays usually deal with problems or topics of concern, and the introduction to an essay tries to place these in context:

un problème qui touche toutes les couches sociales

a problem that affects all levels of society

ce problème est au premier plan de nos préoccupations

this problem is uppermost in our minds

un thème brûlant de l'actualité *a burning issue of the moment*

un problème fort difficile à résoudre *a very difficult problem to solve*

une question qui provoque bien des controverses

a question that causes a great deal of controversy

ce problème a été rendu plus aigu par *this problem has been made more acute by*

le coût social est astronomique *the social cost is astronomical*

un problème dont il est souvent question *a recurring problem*

l'importance de ce phénomène ne peut être sous-estimée

the importance of this phenomenon cannot be over-stated

une des plus grandes menaces qui pèsent sur le monde

one of the biggest threats facing the world

tout est en train de se transformer en profondeur, à un rythme accéléré

everything is changing vastly, at a quickening pace

le problème a pris une telle ampleur que *the problem has reached such proportions that*

le point de non-retour est dépassé *the point of no-return has been passed*

les événements prennent une tournure tragique

events are taking a tragic turn for the worse

il ne faut pas se masquer la réalité *we mustn't hide from reality*

la situation ne cesse pas de se dégrader *the situation keeps getting worse*

les origines du problème résident dans *the roots of the problem lie in*

nous vivons dans un monde où *we live in a world where*

le problème est beaucoup plus sérieux qu'on ne se l'imagine

the problem is much more serious than people think

2 Introductions should indicate the course that the essay will take:

cette dissertation a pour but de *this essay aims to*

j'ai pour objet de présenter et d'analyser les faits

my aim is to present and analyse the facts

pour avoir une vision plus précise de la situation

to obtain a clearer picture of the position

on va examiner les avantages et les inconvénients de

we shall examine the advantages and the disadvantages of

j'essaierai de déterminer les causes principales de

I shall try to determine the main causes of

il faut d'abord définir les idées clés, c'est-à-dire

the key ideas must first of all be defined, namely

3 A paragraph may usefully begin or end with a rhetorical question, to which a suggested answer is then provided:

Comment, alors, traiter le problème de... ? *How then shall we deal with the problem of ... ?*

Comment inverser cette tendance? *How can we reverse this trend?*

Peut-on remédier aux difficultés de... ? *Can we put right the difficulties of ... ?*

Est-il possible de généraliser? *Is it possible to generalise?*

Quelles solutions pourrait-on envisager? *What solutions might be borne in mind?*

Est-ce qu'on peut dire que... ? *Can we say that ... ?*

De quoi s'agit-il en fait? *What in fact is at issue?*

Tout dépend-il de... ? *Does everything depend on ... ?*

Comment aborder un problème qui... ? *How can we tackle a problem that ... ?*

Dans quelle mesure peut-on attribuer... ? *How far can we attribute ... ?*

4 Phrases to start off a paragraph in the main body of the essay could include:

en guise d'introduction *by way of an introduction*

réfléchissons d'abord à *let's first consider*

pour approfondir la question *to go into the matter in more depth*

dans l'état actuel des choses *the way things stand at the moment*

il faut en venir maintenant à *we must now turn to*

comme point de départ on pourrait *as a starting point we could*

l'une des conséquences les plus évidentes est *one of the most obvious consequences is*

un autre aspect du problème est que	*another side of the problem is*
sur le plan humain, il faut considérer	*on a human level we must consider*
pour commencer, il serait utile de	*to start off it would be useful to*
une des premières questions qui se posent	*one of the first questions that arises*
en ce qui concerne	*as far as ... is concerned*
il faut également faire mention de	*mention must also be made of*
en premier lieu examinons	*to start off with let's examine*
pour tirer l'affaire au clair	*to clarify the matter*

5 Ideas about how to solve the problem may well be put forward:

le problème ne peut être traité qu'au niveau de	
	the problem can only be dealt with at the level of
il faut mener une action d'envergure nationale	*we must take action on a national scale*
l'autre solution est de	*the other solution is to*
la clé du problème est	*the key to the problem is*
pour que ce fléau cesse de s'étendre, il faut	*to stop this scourge spreading we must*
mettre sur pied un système au moyen duquel on peut	*to set up a system whereby we can*
ce ne serait pas une mauvaise idée de	*it wouldn't be a bad idea to*
on pourrait envisager de	*we could contemplate*
ceci est sans doute dû en partie à	*this is no doubt partly due to the fact that*
une solution facile qui s'impose	*one vital, easy solution*
ce problème tire ses origines dans	*this problem has its roots in*

6 You may wish to show your or other people's strong views about the topic:

il est scandaleux de	*it is scandalous to*
il serait abusif de	*it would be putting it a bit strongly to*
il n'est pas question de	*it's not a matter of*
ce serait de la folie de	*it would be madness to*
c'est une politique vouée à l'échec	*it's a policy that is bound to fail*
contrairement à ce que l'on croit généralement	*contrary to popular belief*
ce qu'il y a de certain, c'est que	*what is certain is that*
il est fortement déconseillé de	*it is highly inadvisable to*
la société ne peut pas tolérer	*society cannot tolerate*

il est hors de question que	*it's out of the question that*
il ne fait aucun doute que	*there's no doubt that*
on exagérerait à peine en disant que	*it would scarcely be an exaggeration to say that*
la vérité est que	*the fact of the matter is that*
il importe de comprendre que	*it is vital to realise that*
il faut s'élever contre	*one must object to*
il ne saurait être question de	*there can be no question of*
le facteur le plus important est que	*the most important factor is that*
loin de résoudre le problème, cela pourrait	*far from solving the problem, that could*
cette ligne de conduite court le risque de	*this course of action runs the risk of*
on ne peut manquer d'être frappé par	*one cannot help but be struck by*

7 It may be that you know what needs to be done:

cela aurait pour conséquence de	*that would have the result of*
entamer des mesures concrètes	*to initiate concrete measures*
il incombe au gouvernement de	*it is up to the government to*
il conviendrait de	*it would be right to*
une mesure d'importance primordiale	*a step of supreme importance*
pour résoudre les problèmes soulevés, il faut	*to solve the problems raised it is necessary to*

8 Of course, you may not have clear-cut ideas or solutions:

il n'est pas aisé de se forger une opinion	*it isn't easy to form a clear opinion*
certains soutiennent que	*some people maintain that*
les avis sont partagés sur	*opinions are divided over*
il est à prévoir que	*the likely outcome is that*
il reste à savoir si	*it remains to be seen whether*
on voit mal comment	*it is hard to see how*
il pourrait y avoir	*there could well be*
tout semble indiquer que	*everything seems to point to the fact that*
il est difficile de ne pas succomber à	*it's hard not to give in to*
personne n'a réussi à trouver la solution miracle	
	nobody has yet come up with the miracle solution

il ne faut pas s'attendre à une percée spectaculaire

we cannot expect a spectacular breakthrough

il est illusoire de penser que *it's wishful thinking that*

cela met en doute *that calls into question*

le phénomène paraît difficilement explicable *it seems hard to explain the phenomenon*

dépasser la compétence de *to exceed the capabilities of*

9 Whatever your views, the opposite side of the argument needs to be given an airing:

regardons de plus près le revers de la médaille

let's look closely at the other side of the coin

il faut bien reconnaître que *it must be recognised that*

la contrepartie de *the opposing view of*

l'un n'exclut pas l'autre *the one does not exclude the other*

tomber dans l'excès inverse *to go to the opposite extreme*

il en est de même pour *the same thing applies to*

venons-en maintenant à *let us now turn to*

selon les antagonistes de ce point de vue *according to opponents of this point of view*

d'autres faits qui méritent d'être mentionnés sont

other facts which deserve a mention are

un autre argument frappant souvent avancé *another striking argument often put forward*

10 And you need to sum up and reach a reasoned conclusion of some sort:

quelles conclusions tirer de... ? *what conclusions can be reached from ... ?*

tout semble indiquer que *everything would seem to point to the fact that*

tout pousse à croire que *everything leads us to believe that*

à en juger par *to judge by*

on ne peut pas se contenter de *we cannot be satisfied with/we cannot just*

il faut garder un sens des perspectives *we must keep things in perspective*

être# à même de *to be in a position to*

être# en bonne voie de *to be well on the way to*

il est évident, d'après ce qui précède, que *it is clear from all of the above, that*

c'est un phénomène de mode *it's a passing phase*

il s'ensuit que	*it follows from this that*
on est tenté de conclure que	*it is tempting to conclude that*
on pourrait bien se demander si	*one might well wonder whether*
en fin de compte	*when all's said and done*
toutes choses considérées	*all things considered*
en définitive	*when all the arguments have been heard*

Mots et phrases de liaison

à jamais	*for ever*
à tel point que	*to such an extent that*
absolument	*absolutely*
actuellement	*now*
apparemment	*apparently*
approximativement	*approximately*
au contraire	*on the contrary*
au fond	*basically*
autrefois	*in the past*
autrement	*otherwise*
bien entendu	*naturally*
bref	*in short*
cependant	*however*
certainement	*certainly*
complètement	*completely*
considérablement	*considerably*
d'ailleurs	*moreover*
dans un sens	*in one sense*
davantage	*more*
de plus	*furthermore*
de toute façon	*in any case*
désormais	*from now on*
du moins	*at least*
effectivement	*in fact*
en aucun cas	*on no account*
en fait	*actually*
en moyenne	*on average*
en outre	*besides*
en principe	*in theory*
en revanche	*in vain*
évidemment	*obviously*
généralement	*generally*
heureusement	*luckily*
là-dessus	*thereupon*
naguère	*recently*
naturellement	*understandably*
néanmoins	*nevertheless*
notamment	*in particular*
or	*now then*
par conséquent	*as a result*
par contre	*on the other hand*
par la suite	*subsequently*
parfois	*sometimes*
pourtant	*however*
principalement	*mainly*
probablement	*probably*
quant à	*as for*
quelquefois	*sometimes*
sinon	*if not*
soi-disant	*so-called*
surtout	*especially*
tandis que	*whereas*
théoriquement	*theoretically*
totalement	*totally*
tout à fait	*quite, totally*
vice versa	*vice versa*
vraiment	*really*
vraisemblablement	*probably*

LES VERBES SUIVIS D'UN INFINITIF

All the following verbs take an infinitive (e.g. elle s'arrête de manger, il préfère attendre, je commence par écrire, etc.)

accepter de	*to agree to*
s'acharner à	*to be bent on*
achever# de	*to finish*
s'adonner à	*to devote oneself to*
adorer	*to love*
aider à	*to help to*
ambitionner de	*to seek to*
s'amuser à	*to enjoy*
s'appliquer à	*to apply oneself to*
apprendre# à	*to learn to*
s'apprêter à	*to get ready to*
s'arrêter de	*to stop*
arriver à	*to manage to*
s'attendre à	*to expect to*
avoir# du mal à	*to have difficulty in*
avoir# envie de	*to want to*
avoir# l'intention de	*to intend to*
avoir# le droit de	*to have the right to*
avoir# raison de	*to be right to*
avoir# tendance à	*to tend to*
avoir# tort de	*to be wrong to*
brûler de	*to long to*
cesser de	*to stop*
chercher à	*to attempt to*
choisir de	*to choose to*
commencer# à	*to start to*

commencer# par	*to start by*
compter	*to plan to*
consentir# à	*to consent to*
consister en	*to consist of*
se contenter de	*to content oneself with*
continuer à	*to continue to*
contribuer à	*to contribute to*
décider de	*to decide to*
se décider à	*to make up one's mind to*
se dépêcher de	*to hurry to*
désirer	*to wish to*
détester	*to hate to*
devoir#	*to have to*
empêcher de	*to prevent from*
s'empresser de	*to be anxious to, to hasten to*
encourager# à	*to encourage to*
s'engager# à	*to undertake to*
espérer#	*to hope to*
essayer# de	*to try to*
éviter de	*to avoid*
être# en train de	*to be in the process of*
être# sur le point de	*to be about to*
exceller à	*to excel in*
finir de	*to finish*
finir par	*to end up by, to finally ...*
forcer# à	*to force to*
s'habituer à	*to get used to*
hésiter à	*to hesitate to*
s'impatienter de	*to long to*
inciter à	*to urge to*
s'intéresser à	*to be interested in*

inviter à	*to invite to*	prier de	*to beg to*
se lasser de	*to be tired of*	promettre# de	*to promise to*
menacer# de	*to threaten to*	proposer de	*to suggest*
mériter de	*to deserve to*	refuser de	*to refuse to*
mettre# (une heure) à		regretter de	*to regret*
	to take (one hour) to	renoncer# à	*to give up*
se mettre# à	*to start to*	se résigner à	*to be resigned to*
négliger# de	*to neglect to*	se résoudre# à	
nier de	*to deny*		*to make up one's mind to*
obliger# à	*to compel to*	réussir à	*to succeed in*
s'occuper de	*to deal with*	rêver de	*to dream of*
offrir# de	*to offer to*	risquer de	*to risk*
omettre# de	*to omit to*	savoir#	*to know how to*
s'opposer à	*to oppose*	sembler	*to seem to*
oser	*to dare to*	servir à	*to be used as/for*
oublier de	*to forget to*	songer# à	*to consider*
parler de	*to talk about*	souhaiter	*to wish to*
parvenir# à	*to manage to*	tâcher de	*to try to*
penser	*to intend*	tarder à	*to be slow to*
perdre# du temps à	*to waste time*	tenir# à	*to be keen to*
persister à	*to persist in*	tenter de	*to try to*
se plaire# à	*to delight in*	trembler de	*to be afraid to*
préférer#	*to prefer to*	venir# de	*to have just*
prévoir# de	*to plan on*	viser à	*to aim/intend to*